Ward Lock Educational Lives
General Editor: Richard Adams

The aim of this series is to present men and women of both past and present through their own words and those of their contemporaries. Each book sets out to portray the life, achievements, character and thinking of an individual whose career is of relevance and interest to readers – especially teenage readers – of today.

A Portrait of Elizabeth I Roger Pringle
The Brontës Robert L. Wilson
The Adventures of Gavin Maxwell Richard Adams

The Brontës

compiled, edited and introduced by Robert L. Wilson

Ward Lock Educational

Editorial notes © Robert L. Wilson
ISBN 0 7062 3897 4 hardback
ISBN 0 7062 3977 6 paperback

Illustration research and design by Ikon
25, St Pancras Way, London NW1

Set in Monophoto Ehrhardt and printed by
BAS Printers Limited, Over Wallop, Hampshire

for Ward Lock Educational
116 Baker Street, London W1M 2BB
A member of the Pentos Group
Made in Great Britain

Title page: Top Withens

Contents

Introduction

When we speak of 'the Brontës' we mean the three Brontë sisters, Charlotte, Emily and Anne, their brother, Patrick Branwell and their father, the Rev Patrick Brontë. From their earliest years the Brontë children lived at Haworth, on the bleak Yorkshire moors, where their father was Parson. Indeed, Haworth Parsonage was to be their home all their lives: Branwell and Emily both died there in 1848; Charlotte was married from there in 1854 and died in the parsonage in 1855 and their father, Patrick, surviving all his children, remained Minister of Haworth until his death in 1861. Only Anne does not lie in the churchyard at Haworth for, in a vain attempt to prolong her life and fend off the tuberculosis that eventually claimed all the Brontë children, she was taken to Scarborough in 1849 where she died a few days after her arrival there.

There is a tendency, when contemplating the lives of the members of this family for us to emphasize their early deaths and the sadness which affected them all. Yet, against the tragedy must be set the imaginative vitality and creative achievement of the three sisters. It is true that the brother, Branwell, wrote nothing worthy of publishing but he did, during his childhood, participate with his sisters in an extraordinary and joyfully shared world of the imagination. Together they invented lands, people and events and wrote copiously about them. These were the springs from which were to come the novels and poetry of Charlotte, Emily and Anne. How much stimulus was given to them by Branwell is difficult to assess but, since he was particularly close to Emily, it is just possible that *Wuthering Heights* owes something to his influence.

Anne was perhaps the least distinguished of the three sisters. She wrote two novels: *Agnes Grey*, published in 1847 along with *Wuthering Heights*, and *The Tenant of Wildfell Hall*, published in 1848. For sheer originality of conception and imaginative force, we must turn to the poetry of Emily and to her one novel, *Wuthering Heights*, of which Charlotte herself wrote, 'It is rustic all through. It is moorish, and wild, and knotty as a root of heath. Nor was it natural that it should be otherwise; the author herself being a native and nursling of the moors.'

It is, however, Charlotte upon whom any narrative of the lives of the Brontës must focus. She wrote more than the others, publishing *Jane Eyre* in 1847, *Shirley* in 1849 and *Villette* in 1853. An early novel, *The Professor*, was published after her death and she contributed a considerable quantity of verse to the poetry volume published by the three sisters in 1846. She took the initiative in all their ventures and she also lived longer than her brother and sisters and, having once emerged from the anonymity of publishing under the pseudonym of Currer Bell, she became, to a limited extent, a literary celebrity, known to other significant writers of her day, corresponding with them, and moving on occasions in London society. Furthermore, Charlotte was more outgoing than her sisters and at school she made two close friends with whom she corresponded throughout her life. These close friends, Ellen Nussey and Mary Taylor, were still alive when Mrs Gaskell began to collect material for her famous biography of Charlotte which was published in 1857, only two years after Charlotte's death. Both Ellen Nussey and Mary Taylor gave Mrs Gaskell lengthy accounts of their friendship with Charlotte and, even more important, they made available to her biographer many letters which Charlotte had written.

Through the letters and diaries of the Brontës and through the accounts of those who knew and respected them we are able now to trace the story of their lives, coloured by pain, bereavement and sorrow, it is true, but yet shot through with courage, love and a rich and vibrant imaginative power.

1 Childhood and schooldays 1820–1832

Our account of the lives of the Brontës begins with the removal of the family to Haworth in Yorkshire on February 25th 1820. The Rev Patrick Brontë had been appointed Parson and the family moved into Haworth Parsonage. There were five daughters and one son and the eldest, Maria, was only six years old. After her came Elizabeth, Charlotte, Patrick Branwell (the only son), Emily and Anne.

Haworth Parsonage is . . . an oblong stone house, facing down the hill on which the village stands, and with the front door right opposite to the western door of the church, distant about a hundred yards. Of this space twenty yards or so in depth are occupied by the grassy garden, which is scarcely wider than the house. The graveyard lies on two sides of the house and garden. The house consists of four rooms on each floor, and is two stories high. When the Brontës took possession they made the larger parlour, to the left of the entrance, the family sitting-room, while that on the right was appropriated to Mr Brontë as a study. Behind this was the kitchen; behind the former, a sort of flagged store room. Upstairs were four bed-chambers of similar size, with the addition of a small apartment over the passage, or 'lobby', as we call it in the north. This was to the front, the staircase going up right opposite to the entrance. There is the pleasant old fashion of window seats all through the house; and one can see that the parsonage was built in the days when wood was plentiful, as the massive stair banisters, and the wainscots, and the heavy window frames testify.

This little extra upstairs room was appropriated to the children. Small as it was, it was not called a nursery; indeed, it had not the comfort of a fireplace in it; the servants – two affectionate, warm-hearted sisters, who cannot now speak of the family without tears – called the room the 'children's study'. The age of the eldest student was perhaps by this time seven. . . .

From their first going to Haworth their walks were directed rather out towards the heathery moors, sloping upwards behind the parsonage, than towards the long descending village street. A good old woman, who came to nurse Mrs Brontë in the illness – an internal cancer – which grew and gathered upon her, not many months after her arrival at Haworth, tells me that at that time the six little creatures used to walk out, hand in hand, towards the glorious wild moors, which in after days they loved so passionately; the elder ones taking thoughtful care for the toddling wee things.

They were grave and silent beyond their years; subdued, probably, by the presence of serious illness in the house; for, at the time which my informant speaks of, Mrs Brontë was confined to the bedroom from which she never came forth alive. 'You would not have known there was a child in the house, they were such still, noiseless, good little creatures. Maria would shut herself up' (Maria, but seven!) 'in the children's study

Haworth Parsonage at the time of the Brontës

with a newspaper and be able to tell one everything when she came out; debates in Parliament, and I don't know what all. She was as good as a mother to her sisters and brother. But there never were such good children. I used to think them spiritless, they were so different from any children I had ever seen. They were good little creatures. Emily was the prettiest.'

Mrs Brontë was . . . very ill, suffering great pain, but seldom if ever complaining; at her better times begging her nurse to raise her in bed to let her see her clean the grate, 'because she did it as it was done in Cornwall'; devotedly fond of her husband, who warmly repaid her affection, and suffered no one else to take the night-nursing; but, according to my informant, the mother was not very anxious to see much of her children, probably because the sight of them, knowing how soon they were to be left motherless, would have agitated her too much. So the little things clung quietly together, for their father was busy in his study and in his parish, or with their mother, and they took their meals alone; sat reading, or whispering low, in the 'children's study', or wandered out on the hillside, hand in hand. . . .

Mrs Brontë died in September 1821, and the lives of those quiet children must have become quieter and lonelier still. Charlotte tried hard, in after years, to recall the remembrance of her mother, and could bring back two or three pictures of her. One was when, some time in the evening light, she had been playing with her little boy, Patrick Branwell, in the parlour of Haworth Parsonage. But the recollections of four or five years old are of a very fragmentary character.

Owing to some illness of the digestive organs Mr Brontë was obliged to be very careful about his diet; and, in order to avoid temptation, and possibly to have the quiet necessary for digestion, he had begun, before his wife's death, to take his dinner alone – a habit which he always retained. He did not require companionship; therefore he did not seek it, either in his walks or in his daily life. The quiet regularity of his domestic hours was only broken in upon by churchwardens, and visitors on parochial business; and sometimes by a neighbouring clergyman, who came down the hills, across the moors, to mount up again to Haworth Parsonage, and spend an evening there. But, owing to Mrs Brontë's death so soon after her husband had removed into the district, and also to the distances, and the bleak country to be traversed, the wives of these clerical friends did not accompany their husbands; and the daughters grew up out of childhood into girlhood bereft, in a singular manner, of all such society as would have been natural to their age, sex, and station.

The Reverend Patrick Brontë as a young man and in old age

The Parlour of the Parsonage

But the children did not want society. To small infantine gaieties they were unaccustomed. They were all in all to each other. I do not suppose that there ever was a family more tenderly bound to each other. Maria read the newspapers, and reported intelligence to her younger sisters which it is wonderful they could take an interest in. But I suspect that they had no 'children's books', and that their eager minds 'browsed undisturbed among the wholesome pasturage of English literature', as Charles Lamb expresses it. The servants of the household appear to have been much impressed with the little Brontës' extraordinary cleverness. In a letter which I had from him on this subject their father writes, 'The servants often said that they had never seen such a clever little girl' (as Charlotte), 'and that they were obliged to be on their guard as to what they said and did before her. Yet she and the servants always lived on good terms with each other.'

from *The Life of Charlotte Brontë* by Mrs Gaskell

Mrs Gaskell quotes further from this letter written to her by the Rev Patrick Brontë:

'When mere children, as soon as they could read and write, Charlotte and her brother and sisters used to invent and act little plays of their own, in which the Duke of Wellington, my daughter Charlotte's hero, was sure to come off conqueror; when a dispute would not unfrequently arise amongst them regarding the comparative merits of him, Buonaparte, Hannibal, and Cæsar. When the argument got warm, and rose to its height, as their mother was then dead, I had sometimes to come in as arbitrator, and settle the dispute according to the best of my judgment. Generally, in the management of these concerns, I frequently thought that I discovered signs of rising talent, which I had seldom or never before seen in any of their age. . . . A circumstance now occurs to my mind which I may as well mention. When my children were very young, when, as far as I can remember, the oldest was about ten years of age, and the youngest about four, thinking that they knew more than I had yet discovered, in order to make them speak with less timidity, I deemed that if they were put under a sort of cover I might gain my end; and happening to have a mask in the house, I told them all to stand back and speak boldly from under cover of the mask.

'I began with the youngest (Anne, afterwards Acton Bell), and asked what a child like her most wanted; she answered, "Age and experience". I asked the next (Emily, afterwards Ellis Bell) what I had best do with her brother, Branwell, who was sometimes a naughty boy; she answered, "Reason with him, and when he won't listen to reason whip him". I asked Branwell what was the best way of knowing the difference between the intellects of man and woman; he answered, "By considering the difference between them as to their bodies". I then asked Charlotte what was the best book in the world; she answered, "The Bible". And what was the next best; she answered, "The Book of Nature". I then asked the next what was the best mode of education for a woman; she answered, "That which would make her rule her house well". Lastly, I asked the oldest what was the best mode of spending time; she answered, "By laying it out in preparation for a happy eternity". I may not have given precisely their words, but I have nearly done so, as they made a deep and lasting impression on my memory. The substance, however, was exactly what I have stated.'

The strange and quaint simplicity of the mode taken by the father to ascertain the hidden characters of his children, and the tone and character of these questions and answers, show the curious education which was made by the circumstances surrounding the Brontës. They knew no other children. They knew no other modes of thought than what were suggested to them by the fragments of clerical conversation which they overheard in the parlour, or the subjects of village and local interest which they heard discussed in the kitchen. Each had its own strong characteristic flavour.

They took a vivid interest in the public characters, and the local and foreign as well as home politics discussed in the newspapers. Long before Maria Brontë died, at the age of eleven, her father used to say he could converse with her on any of the leading topics of the day with as much freedom and pleasure as with any grown-up person.

In July 1824, the two oldest daughters were sent to a boarding school for the daughters of clergymen at Cowan Bridge, a small hamlet on the coach road between Leeds and Kendal. A few months later, Charlotte and Emily joined them. Charlotte used her memories of this school in those chapters of *Jane Eyre* which describe life at Lowood School. Here are some extracts from that section of the novel.

The next day commenced as before, getting up and dressing by rush-light; but this morning we were obliged to dispense with the ceremony of washing: the water in the pitchers was frozen. A change had taken place in the weather the preceding evening, and a keen north-east wind, whistling through the crevices of our bedroom windows all night long, had made us shiver in our beds, and turned the contents of the ewers to ice.

Before the long hour and a half of prayers and Bible reading was over, I felt ready to perish with cold. Breakfast-time came at last, and this morning the porridge was not burnt; the quality was eatable, the quantity small; how small my portion seemed! I wished it had been doubled.

In the course of the day I was enrolled a member of the fourth class, and regular tasks and occupations were assigned me: hitherto, I had only been a spectator of the proceedings at Lowood, I was now to become an actor therein. At first, being little accustomed to learn by heart, the lessons appeared to me both long and difficult: the frequent change from task to task, too, bewildered me; and I was glad, when, about three o'clock in the afternoon, Miss Smith put into my hands a border of muslin two yards long, together with needle, thimble, &c., and sent me to sit in a quiet corner of the schoolroom, with directions to hem the same.

Cowan Bridge Boarding School for the daughters of clergymen

At that hour most of the others were sewing likewise; but one class still stood round Miss Scatcherd's chair reading, and as all was quiet, the subject of their lessons could be heard, together with the manner in which each girl acquitted herself, and the animadversions or commendations of Miss Scatcherd on the performance. It was English history: among the readers, I observed my acquaintance of the verandah: at the commencement of the lesson, her place had been at the top of the class, but for some error of pronunciation or some inattention to stops, she was suddenly sent to the very bottom. Even in that obscure position, Miss Scatcherd continued to make her an object of constant notice: she was continually addressing to her such phrases as the following:–

'Burns' (such it seems was her name: the girls here were all called by their surnames, as boys are elsewhere), 'Burns, you are standing on the side of your shoe, turn your toes out immediately.' 'Burns, you poke your chin out most unpleasantly, draw it in.' 'Burns, I insist on your holding your head up: I will not have you before me in that attitude,' &c., &c.

A chapter having been read through twice, the books were closed and the girls examined. The lesson had comprised part of the reign of Charles I., and there were sundry questions about tonnage and poundage, and ship-money, which most of them appeared unable to answer; still, every little difficulty was solved instantly when it reached Burns: her memory seemed to have retained the substance of the whole lesson, and she was ready with answers on every point. I kept expecting that Miss Scatcherd would praise her attention; but, instead of that, she suddenly cried out:–

'You dirty, disagreeable girl! you have never cleaned your nails this morning!'

Burns made no answer: I wondered at her silence.

'Why,' thought I, 'does she not explain that she could neither clean her nails nor wash her face, as the water was frozen?'

My attention was now called off by Miss Smith desiring me to hold a skein of thread: while she was winding it, she talked to me from time to time, asking whether I had ever been at school before, whether I could mark, stitch, knit, &c.; till she dismissed me, I could not pursue my observations on Miss Scatcherd's movements. When I returned to my seat, that lady was just delivering an order, of which I did not catch the import; but Burns immediately left the class, and, going into the small inner room where the books were kept, returned in half a minute, carrying in her hand a bundle of twigs tied together at one end. This ominous tool she presented to Miss Scatcherd with a respectful curtsy; then she quietly, and without being told, unloosed her pinafore, and the teacher instantly and sharply inflicted on her neck a dozen strokes with the bunch of twigs. Not a tear rose to Burns' eye; and, while I paused from my sewing, because my fingers quivered at this spectacle with a sentiment of unavailing and impotent anger, not a feature of her pensive face altered its ordinary expression.

'Hardened girl!' exclaimed Miss Scatcherd; 'nothing can correct you of your slatternly habits: carry the rod away.'

Burns obeyed: I looked at her narrowly as she emerged from the book-closet; she was just putting back her handkerchief into her pocket, and the trace of a tear glistened on her thin cheek. . . .

*   *   *

My first quarter at Lowood seemed an age; and not the golden age either: it comprised an irksome struggle with difficulties in habituating myself to new rules and unwonted tasks. The fear of failure in these points harassed me worse than the physical hardships of my lot; though these were not trifles.

During January, February, and part of March, the deep snows, and, after their melting, the almost impassable roads, prevented our stirring beyond the garden walls, except to go to church; but within these limits we had to pass an hour every day in the open air. Our clothing was insufficient to protect us from the severe cold: we had no boots, the snow got into our shoes and melted there; our ungloved hands became numbed and covered with chilblains, as were our feet: I remember well the distracting irritation I endured from this cause every evening, when my feet inflamed; and the torture of thrusting the swelled, raw, and stiff toes into my shoes in the morning. Then the scanty supply of food was distressing: with the keen appetites of growing children, we had scarcely sufficient to keep alive a delicate invalid. From this deficiency of nourishment resulted an abuse, which pressed hardly on the younger pupils: whenever the famished great girls had an opportunity, they would coax or menace the little ones out of their portion. Many a time I have shared between two claimants the precious morsel of brown bread distributed at tea-time; and after relinquishing to a third, half the contents of my mug of coffee, I have swallowed the remainder with an accompaniment of secret tears, forced from me by the exigency of hunger.

Sundays were dreary days in that wintry season. We had to walk two miles to Brocklebridge Church, where our patron officiated. We set out cold, we arrived at church colder: during the morning service we became almost paralysed. It was too far to return to dinner, and an allowance of cold meat and bread, in the same penurious proportion observed in our ordinary meals, was served round between the services.

At the close of the afternoon service we returned by an exposed and hilly road, where the bitter winter wind, blowing over a range of snowy summits to the north, almost flayed the skin from our faces.

I can remember Miss Temple walking lightly and rapidly along our drooping line, her plaid cloak, which the frosty wind fluttered, gathered close about her, and encouraging us, by precept and example, to keep up our spirits, and march forward, as she said, 'like stalwart soldiers'. The other teachers, poor things, were generally themselves too much dejected to attempt the task of cheering others.

How we longed for the light and heat of a blazing fire when we got back! But, to the little ones at least, this was denied: each hearth in the schoolroom was immediately surrounded by a double row of great girls, and behind them the younger children crouched in groups, wrapping their starved arms in their pinafores.

One memorable incident from *Jane Eyre* reveals the strict, repressive and hypocritical puritanism of the founder of the school, Mr Brocklehurst.

Meantime, Mr Brocklehurst, standing on the hearth with his hands behind his back, majestically surveyed the whole school. Suddenly his eye gave a blink, as if it had met something that either dazzled or shocked its pupil; turning, he said in more rapid accents than he had hitherto used:– 'Miss Temple, Miss Temple, what – *what* is that girl with curled hair? Red hair, ma'am, curled – curled all over?' And extending his cane he pointed to the awful object, his hand shaking as he did so.

'It is Julia Severn,' replied Miss Temple, very quietly.

'Julia Severn, ma'am! And why has she, or any other, curled hair? Why, in defiance of every precept and principle of this house, does she conform to the world so openly – here in an evangelical, charitable establishment – as to wear her hair one mass of curls?'

'Julia's hair curls naturally,' returned Miss Temple, still more quietly.

'Naturally! Yes, but we are not to conform to nature: I wish these girls to be the children of Grace: and why that abundance? I have again and again intimated that I desire the hair to be arranged closely, modestly, plainly. Miss Temple, that girl's hair must be cut off entirely; I will send a barber to-morrow: and I see others who have far too much of the excrescence – that tall girl, tell her to turn round. Tell all the first form to rise up and direct their faces to the wall.'

Miss Temple passed her handkerchief over her lips, as if to smooth away the involuntary smile that curled them; she gave the order, however, and when the first class could take in what was required of them, they obeyed. Leaning a little back on my bench, I could see the looks and grimaces with which they commented on this manoeuvre: it was a pity Mr Brocklehurst could not see them too; he would perhaps have felt that, whatever he might do with the outside of the cup and platter, the inside was further beyond his interference than he imagined.

He scrutinised the reverse of these living medals some five minutes, then pronounced sentence. These words fell like the knell of doom :– 'All those top-knots must be cut off.'

Miss Temple seemed to remonstrate.

'Madam,' he pursued, 'I have a master to serve whose kingdom is not of this world: my mission is to mortify in these girls the lusts of the flesh; to teach them to clothe themselves with shamefacedness and sobriety, not with braided hair and costly apparel; and each of the young persons before us has a string of hair twisted in plaits which vanity itself might have woven: these, I repeat, must be cut off; think of the time wasted, of——'

Mr Brocklehurst was here interrupted: three other visitors, ladies, now entered the room. They ought to have come a little sooner to have heard his lecture on dress, for they were splendidly attired in velvet, silk, and furs. The two younger of the trio (fine girls of sixteen and seventeen) had grey beaver hats, then in fashion, shaded with ostrich plumes, and from under the brim of this graceful head-dress fell a profusion of light tresses, elaborately curled; the elder lady was enveloped in a costly velvet shawl, trimmed with ermine, and she wore a false front of French curls.

These ladies were deferentially received by Miss Temple, as Mrs and the Misses Brocklehurst, and conducted to seats of honour at the top of the room. It seems they had come in the carriage with their reverend relative, and had been conducting a rummaging scrutiny of the rooms upstairs, while he transacted business with the housekeeper, questioned the laundress, and lectured the superintendent.

It is possible that Charlotte exaggerated her memories of Cowan Bridge School for perfectly justifiable literary reasons. However, we have the opinion of the Rev Angus M. Mackay who, in 1894, published an article on the founder of the school,

the Rev W. Carus Wilson, in which he examined various books and tracts written by Wilson. Here is an extract from Mackay's article.

It has been questioned whether the whipping scene in *Jane Eyre* represented a fact, and whether Mr Carus Wilson could ever have advised the teachers 'to punish the body to save the soul'. But these books, both as regards illustrations and letterpress, seem, as one glances through, to bristle with canes and rods, and Mr Wilson frequently insists on the necessity of corporal punishment. I quote one of his anecdotes because it seems to refer to some girl at Cowan Bridge. 'A poor little girl who had been taken into a school was whipped. She asked, "If they love us, why do they whip us?" A little girl of six replied, "It is because they love us, and it is to make us remember what a sad thing sin is. God would be angry with them if they did not whip us".'

No one, I am sure, could read Mr Carus Wilson's *Thoughts Suggested to the Superintendent*, without being astonished at the accuracy with which Charlotte Brontë has represented in *Jane Eyre* his aims and religious ideas. The document – which is earnest in tone – takes us into

The Rev W. Carus Wilson –
thought to be the model for
Mr Brocklehurst in Charlotte's
Jane Eyre

the very atmosphere of Chapter VI *of Jane Eyre*. Every one remembers the scene in which Mr Brocklehurst orders the curls to be cut off, and declares it his mission 'to mortify in these girls the lusts of the flesh, and to teach them to clothe themselves with shamefacedness and sobriety'. In his *Thoughts*, written thirty-three years after Charlotte left Cowan Bridge, Mr Wilson writes: 'The pupils are necessarily put into a very simple and uniform attire. Many of them no doubt feel it. They have been unfortunately accustomed, perhaps, even to excess in this very prevailing and increasing love of dress, for alas, clergymen's families are not exempt from the mania – not even the poorest. With me it was always an object to nip in the bud any growing symptom of vanity.' Mr Brocklehurst everywhere insists that the pupils should be 'made useful and kept humble', and Mr Wilson, in his final manifesto, says that the teacher must discountenance 'trivial and useless work'. The children are to be 'brought up usefully, not tawdrily. . . . The tinsel and the varnish are of little moment compared with excellence in plain, useful work. . . . It will be a sorry look-out for a clergyman's daughter if she is sent out from the school, for instance, a first-rate performer in crochet and worsted work, and that sort of thing – however useful it may be – but unable to cut out and mend her own garments.'

Let me repeat, these extracts – which might be increased indefinitely – are not given for the purpose of reopening the question of Mr Carus Wilson's character. It may be that most people nowadays will think that his lights were dim, and his methods mistaken, but there can be no doubt about his conscientiousness and good intentions. My purpose is only to show how marvellously accurate was the insight into character and the memory for words and incidents of Charlotte Brontë when she was a little girl of eight.

The inadequate food and unhealthy conditions of the school were such that the two oldest Brontë children began to ail.

In the spring of it (the year 1825) Maria became so rapidly worse that Mr Brontë was sent for. He had not previously been aware of her illness, and the condition in which he found her was a terrible shock to him. He took her home in the Leeds coach, the girls crowding out into the road to follow her with their eyes over the bridge, past the cottages, and then out of sight for ever. She died a very few days after her arrival at home. Perhaps the news of her death falling suddenly into the life of which her patient existence had formed a part, only a little week or so before, made those who remained at Cowan Bridge look with more anxiety on Elizabeth's symptoms, which also turned out to be consumptive. She was sent home in charge of a confidential servant of the establishment; and she, too, died in the early summer of that year. Charlotte was thus suddenly called into the responsibilities of eldest sister in a motherless family. She remembered how anxiously her dear sister Maria had striven, in her grave, earnest way, to be a tender helper and a counsellor to them all; and the duties that now fell upon her seemed almost like a legacy from the gentle little sufferer so lately dead.

Both Charlotte and Emily returned to school after the midsummer holidays in this fatal year. But before the next winter it was thought desirable to advise their removal, as it was evident that the damp situation of the house at Cowan Bridge did not suit their health.

Mrs Gaskell

So, between 1825 and 1831, the four remaining children stayed at home in Haworth. About a year after the death of their mother, an aunt, Miss Elizabeth Branwell, had moved to the parsonage to help look after the family.

Elizabeth Branwell – the
Brontë children's Aunt
Branwell

Miss Branwell instructed the children at regular hours in all she could teach, converting her bedchamber into their schoolroom. Their father was in the habit of relating to them any public news in which he felt an interest; and from the opinions of his strong and independent mind they would gather much food for thought; but I do not know whether he gave them any direct instruction. Charlotte's deep, thoughtful spirit appears to have felt almost painfully the tender responsibility which rested upon her with reference to her remaining sisters. She was only eighteen months older than Emily; but Emily and Anne were simply companions and playmates, while Charlotte was motherly friend and guardian to both; and this loving assumption of duties beyond her years made her feel considerably older than she really was.

Patrick Branwell, their only brother, was a boy of remarkable promise, and, in some ways, of extraordinary precocity of talent. Mr Brontë's friends advised him to send his son to school; but, remembering both the strength of will of his own youth and his mode of employing it, he believed that Patrick was better at home, and that he himself could teach him well, as he had taught others before. So Patrick – or, as his family called him, Branwell – remained at Haworth, working hard for some hours a day with his father; but, when the time of the latter was taken up with his parochial duties, the boy was thrown into chance companionship with the lads of the village – for youth will to youth, and boys will to boys.

Still, he was associated in many of his sisters' plays and amusements. These were mostly of a sedentary and intellectual nature. I have had a curious packet confided to me, containing an immense amount of manuscript, in an inconceivably small space – tales, dramas, poems, romances, written principally by Charlotte, in a hand which it is almost impossible to decipher without the aid of a magnifying glass.

Mrs Gaskell

These little manuscripts, written between 1829 and 1845, have since been deciphered. They are a closely connected series of stories, poems, novels, plays and historical accounts all relating to the same fictitious world and concerning the same characters. All four children felt an obsessive urge to elaborate this imaginary world which they shared. It became so powerful an alternative to real life that even in adulthood they remained addicted to it as if it were a drug. Charlotte writes of the origins of this world of day-dream in one of those tiny manuscripts handed to Mrs Gaskell.

THE HISTORY OF THE YEAR 1820

Once papa lent my sister Maria a book. It was an old geography book; she wrote on its blank leaf, 'Papa lent me this book.' This book is a hundred and twenty years old; it is at this moment lying before me. While I write this I am in the kitchen of the Parsonage, Haworth; Tabby, the servant, is washing up the breakfast things, and Anne, my younger sister (Maria was my eldest), is kneeling on a chair, looking at some cakes which Tabby had been baking for us. Emily is in the parlour, brushing the carpet. Papa and Branwell are gone to Keighley. Aunt is upstairs in her room, and I am sitting by the table writing this in the kitchen. Keighley is a small town four miles from here. Papa and Branwell are gone for the newspaper, the 'Leeds Intelligencer', a most excellent Tory newspaper, edited by Mr Wood, and the proprietor, Mr Henneman. We take two and see three newspapers a week. We take the 'Leeds Intelligencer,' Tory, and the 'Leeds Mercury,' Whig, edited by Mr Baines, and his brother, son-in-law, and his two sons, Edward and

A selection of the little books made and written by the Brontë children. The books measure two inches in height and one and half inches in width

A watercolour by Charlotte depicting
The Bay of Glasstown, the main
imaginary city created in the little
books

Drawings of toy soldiers in Branwell's first little book

Talbot. We see the 'John Bull;' it is a high Tory, very violent. Dr Driver lends us it, as likewise 'Blackwood's Magazine,' the most able periodical there is. The editor is Mr Christopher North, an old man seventy-four years of age; the 1st of April is his birthday; his company are Timothy Tickler, Morgan O'Doherty, Macrabin Mordecai, Mullion, Warnell, and James Hogg, a man of most extraordinary genius, a Scottish shepherd. Our plays were established: 'Young Men,' June 1826; 'Our Fellows,' July 1827; 'Islanders,' December 1827. These are our three great plays that are not kept secret. Emily's and my best plays were established December 1, 1827; the others March 1828. Best plays mean secret plays; they are very nice ones. All our plays are very strange ones. Their nature I need not write on paper, for I think I shall always remember them. The 'Young Men's' play took its rise from some wooden soldiers Branwell had; 'Our Fellows' from 'Aesop's Fables'; and the 'Islanders' from several events which happened. I will sketch out the origin of our plays more explicitly if I can. First, 'Young Men.' Papa bought Branwell some wooden soldiers at Leeds; when papa came home it was night, and we were in bed, so next morning Branwell came to our door with a box of soldiers. Emily and I jumped out of bed, and I snatched up one and exclaimed, 'This is the Duke of Wellington! This shall be the Duke!' When I had said this Emily likewise took up one and said it should be hers; when Anne came down she said one should be hers. Mine was the prettiest of the whole, and the tallest, and the most perfect in every part. Emily's was a grave-looking fellow, and we called him 'Gravey'. Anne's was a queer little thing, much like herself, and we called him 'Waiting-boy'. Branwell chose his and called him 'Buonaparte'.

The following extract from the little manuscripts is also by Charlotte, from the introduction to *Tales of the Islanders*.

June the 31st, 1829

The play of the 'Islanders' was formed in December 1827, in the following manner: One night, about the time when the cold sleet and stormy fogs of November are succeeded by the snowstorms, and high, piercing night winds of confirmed winter, we were all sitting round the warm blazing kitchen fire, having just concluded a quarrel with Tabby concerning the propriety of lighting a candle, from which she came off victorious, no candle having been produced. A long pause succeeded, which was at last broken by Branwell saying, in a lazy manner, 'I don't know what to do.' This was echoed by Emily and Anne.

Page from diary of 1837 written by Emily and Anne describing life at the Parsonage

Tabby 'What, ya ma go t' bed.'
Branwell 'I'd rather do anything than that.'
Charlotte 'Why are you so glum to-night, Tabby? Oh! suppose we had each an island of our own.'
Branwell 'If we had I would choose the Island of Man.'
Charlotte 'And I would choose the Isle of Wight.'
Emily 'The Isle of Arran for me.'
Anne 'And mine shall be Guernsey.'

We then chose who should be chief men in our islands. Branwell chose John Bull, Astley Cooper, and Leigh Hunt; Emily, Walter Scott, Mr Lockhart, Johnny Lockhart; Anne, Michael Sadler, Lord Bentinck, Sir Henry Halford. I chose the Duke of Wellington and two sons, Christopher North and Co, and Mr Abernethy. Here our conversation was interrupted by the, to us, dismal sound of the clock striking seven, and we were summoned off to bed. The next day we added many others to our list of men, till we got almost all the chief men of the kingdom. After this, for a long time, nothing worth noticing occurred. In June 1828 we erected a school on a fictitious island, which was to contain 1,000 children.

In January 1831, at the age of fifteen, Charlotte was sent to school again, this time as a pupil to Miss Margaret Wooler who ran a girls' school at Roe Head. Two school companions, Ellen Nussey and Mary Taylor, who were to become life-long friends of Charlotte, have written their accounts of meeting and being with her in school.

Arriving at school about a week after the general assembling of the pupils, I was not expected to accompany them when the time came for their daily exercise, but while they were out, I was led into the school-room, and quietly left to make my observations. I had come to the conclusion it was very nice and comfortable for a school-room, though I had little knowledge of school-rooms in general, when, turning to the window to observe the look-out I became aware for the first time that I was not alone; there was a silent, weeping, dark little figure in the large bay-window; she must, I thought, have risen from the floor. As soon as I had recovered from my surprise, I went from the far end of the room, where the book-shelves were, the contents of which I must have contemplated with a little awe in anticipation of coming studies. A crimson cloth covered the long table down the centre of the room, which helped, no doubt, to hide the shrinking little figure from my view. I was touched and troubled at once to see her so sad and so tearful.

I said *shrinking*, because her attitude, when I saw her, was that of one who wished to hide both herself and her grief. She did not shrink, however, when spoken to, but in very few words confessed she was 'home-sick'. After a little of such comfort as could be offered, it was suggested to her that there was a possibility of her too having to comfort the speaker by and by for the same cause. A faint quivering smile then lighted her face; the tear-drops fell; we silently took each other's hands, and at once we felt that genuine sympathy which always consoles, even though it be unexpressed. We did not talk or stir till we heard the approaching footsteps of other pupils coming in from their play; it had been a game called 'French and English', which was always very vigorously played, but in which Charlotte Brontë never could be induced to join. Perhaps the merry voices contesting for victory, which reached our ears in the school-room, jarred upon her then sensitive misery, and caused her ever after to dislike the game; but she was physically unequal to that exercise of muscle which was keen enjoyment to strong, healthy girls, both older and younger than herself. Miss Wooler's system of education required that a good deal of her pupils' work should be done in classes, and to effect this, new pupils had generally a season of solitary study; but Charlotte's fervent application made this period a very short one to her, – she was quickly up to the needful standard, and ready for the daily routine and arrangement of studies, and as quickly did she outstrip her companions, rising from the bottom of the classes to the top, a position which, when she had once gained, she never had to regain. She was first in everything but play, yet never was a word heard of envy or jealousy from her companions; every one felt she had won her laurels by an amount of diligence and hard labour of which they were incapable. She never exulted in her successes or seemed conscious of them; her mind was so wholly set on attaining knowledge that she apparently forgot all else.

Charlotte's appearance did not strike me at first as it did others. I saw her grief, not herself particularly, till afterwards. She never seemed to me the unattractive little person others designated her, but certainly she was at this time anything but *pretty*; even her good points were lost. Her naturally beautiful hair of soft silky brown being then dry and frizzy-looking, screwed up in tight little curls, showing features that were all the plainer from her exceeding thinness and want of complexion, she looked 'dried in'. A dark, rusty green stuff dress of old-fashioned make detracted still more from her appearance; but let her wear what she might, or do what she would, she had ever the demeanour of a born gentlewoman; vulgarity was an element that never won the slightest affinity with her nature. Some of the elder girls, who had been years at school, thought her ignorant. This was true in one sense; ignorant she was indeed in the elementary education which is given in schools, but she far surpassed her most advanced school-fellows in knowledge of what was passing in the world at large and in the literature of her country. She knew a thousand things in these matters unknown to them.

She had taught herself a little French before she came to school; this little knowledge of the language was very useful to her when afterwards she was engaged in translation or dictation. She soon began to make a good figure in French lessons. Music she wished to acquire, for which she had both ear and taste, but her near-sightedness caused her to stoop so dreadfully in order to see her notes, she was dissuaded from persevering in the acquirement, especially as she had at this time an invincible objection to wearing glasses. Her very tapered fingers, tipped with the most circular nails, did not seem very suited for instrumental execution; but when wielding the pen or the pencil, they appeared in the very office they were created for.

Her appetite was of the smallest; for years she had not tasted animal food; she had the greatest dislike to it; she always had something specially provided for her at our midday repast. Towards the close of the first half-year she was induced to take, by little and little, meat gravy with vegetable, and in the second half-year she commenced taking a very small portion of animal food daily. She then grew a little bit plumper, looked younger and more animated, though she was never what is called lively at this period. She always seemed to feel that a deep responsibility rested upon her; that she was an object of expense to those at home, and that she must use every moment to attain the purpose for which she was sent to school, *i.e.*, to fit herself for governess life. She had almost too much opportunity for her conscientious diligence; we were so little restricted in our doings, the industrious might accomplish the appointed tasks of the day and enjoy a little leisure, but she chose in many things to do *double* lessons when not prevented by class arrangement or a companion. In two of her studies she was associated with her friend, and great was her distress if her companion failed to be ready, when she was, with the lesson of the day. She liked the stated task to be over, that she might be free to pursue her self-appointed ones. Such, however, was her conscientiousness that she never did what some girls think it generous to do; generous

Ellen Nussey drawn by Charlotte   Ellen in later life

Roe Head School drawn by Charlotte. It was here Charlotte met Ellen
Nussey, a fellow pupil who became her lifelong friend and correspondent

and unselfish though she was, she never whispered help to a companion in class (as she might have done) to rid herself of the trouble of having to appear again. All her school-fellows regarded her, I believe, as a model of high rectitude, close application, and great abilities. She did not play or amuse herself when others did. When her companions were merry round the fire, or otherwise enjoying themselves during the twilight, which was always a precious time of relaxation, she would be kneeling close to the window busy with her studies, and this would last so long that she was accused of seeing in the dark; yet though she did not play, as girls style play, she was ever ready to help with suggestions in those plays which required taste or arrangement.

About a month after the assembling of the school, one of the pupils had an illness. There was great competition among the girls for permission to sit with the invalid, but Charlotte was never of the number, though she was as assiduous in kindness and attention as the rest in spare moments; but to sit with the patient was indulgence and leisure, and these she would not permit herself.

It was shortly after this illness that Charlotte caused such a panic of terror by her thrilling relations of the wanderings of a somnambulist. She brought together all the horrors her imagination could create, from surging seas, raging breakers, towering castle walls, high precipices, invisible chasms and dangers. Having wrought these materials to the highest pitch of effect, she brought out, in almost cloud-height, her somnambulist, walking on shaking turrets, – all told in a voice that conveyed more than words alone can express. A shivering terror seized the recovered invalid; a pause ensued; then a subdued cry of pain came from Charlotte herself, with a terrified command to others to call for help. She was in bitter distress. Something like remorse seemed to linger in her mind after this incident; for weeks there was no prevailing upon her to resume her tales, and she never again created terrors for her listeners.
Scribner's Monthly, vol. ii. 1871., 'Reminiscences of Charlotte Brontë', by 'E.'
Reprinted in *The Brontë Society Transactions*, Part x. 1899

Her other friend, Mary Taylor, gave Mrs Gaskell her earliest impression of Charlotte in a letter that she wrote from New Zealand in 1856:

I first saw her coming out of a covered cart, in very old-fashioned clothes, and looking very cold and miserable. She was coming to school at Miss Wooler's. When she appeared in the schoolroom her dress was changed, but just as old. She looked a little, old woman, so short-sighted that she always appeared to be seeking something, and moving her head from side to side to catch a sight of it. She was very shy and nervous, and spoke with a strong Irish accent. When a book was given her she dropped her head over it till her nose nearly touched it, and when she was told to hold her head up, up went the book after it, still close to her nose, so that it was not possible to help laughing. . . .

We used to be furious politicians, as one could hardly help being in 1832. She knew the names of the two Ministries: the one that resigned, and the one that succeeded and passed the Reform Bill. She worshipped the Duke of Wellington, but said that Sir Robert Peel was not to be trusted; he did not act from principle, like the rest, but from expediency. I, being of the furious Radical party, told her, 'How could any of them trust one another? they were all of them rascals!' Then she would launch out into praises of the Duke of Wellington, referring to his actions; which I could not contradict, as I knew nothing about him. She said she had taken interest in politics ever since she was five years old. She did not get her opinions from her father – that is, not directly – but from the papers, etc., he preferred.

She used to speak of her two elder sisters, Maria and Elizabeth, who died at Cowan Bridge. I used to believe them to have been wonders of talent and kindness. She told me, early one morning, that she had just been dreaming: she had been told that she was wanted in the drawing-room, and it was Maria and Elizabeth. I was eager for her to go on, and when she said there was no more, I said, 'But go on! *Make it out!* I know you can.' She said she would not; she wished she had not dreamed, for it did not go on nicely; they were changed; they had forgotten what they used to care for. They were very fashionably dressed, and began criticizing the room, etc.

This habit of 'making out' interests for themselves, that most children get who have none in actual life, was very strong in her. The whole family used to 'make out' histories, and invent characters and events. I told her sometimes they were like growing potatoes in a cellar. She said, sadly, 'Yes! I know we are!'

2 At home and at work 1832–1841

In May 1832, Charlotte left Roe Head and in July we find her describing the pattern of her life back at Haworth to Ellen Nussey:

HAWORTH, July 21st, 1832

MY DEAREST ELLEN, – Your kind and interesting letter gave me the sincerest pleasure. I have been expecting to hear from you almost every day since my arrival at home and I at length began to despair of receiving the wished-for letter. You ask me to give you a description of the manner in which I have passed every day since I left School: this is soon done, as an account of one day is an account of all. In the morning from nine o'clock till half-past twelve, I instruct my Sisters and draw, then we walk till dinner, after dinner I sew till tea time, and after tea I either read, write, do a little fancy work or draw, as I please. Thus in one delightful, though somewhat monotonous course my life is passed. I have only been out to tea twice since I came home. We are expecting company this afternoon and on Tuesday next we shall have all the Female teachers of the Sunday-school to tea. . . .

In the following month, Charlotte and Branwell visited Ellen Nussey who wrote this account of their visit:

Charlotte's first visit from Haworth was made about three months after she left school. She travelled in a two-wheeled gig, the only conveyance to be had in Haworth except the covered cart which brought her to school. Mr Brontë sent Branwell as an escort; he was *then* a very dear brother, as dear to Charlotte as her own soul; they were in perfect accord of taste and feeling, and it was mutual delight to be together.

Branwell probably had never been far from home before! he was in wild ecstasy with everything. He walked about in unrestrained boyish enjoyment, taking views in every direction of the old turret-roofed house,

The Brontë sisters painted by Branwell *c.* 1835. From left to right: Anne, Emily and Charlotte. In the middle is a suggestion of another figure, possibly Branwell

the fine chestnut trees on the lawn (one tree especially interested him because it was 'iron-garthed', having been split by storms, but still flourishing in great majesty), and a large rookery, which gave to the house a good background – all these he noted and commented upon with perfect enthusiasm. He told his sister he 'was leaving her in Paradise, and if she were not intensely happy she never would be!' Happy, indeed, she then was, *in himself*, for she, with her own enthusiasms, looked forward to what her brother's great promise and talent might effect. He would at this time be between fifteen and sixteen years of age.

The visit passed without much to mark it (at this distance of time) except that we crept away together from household life as much as we could. Charlotte liked to pace the plantations or seek seclusion in the fruit garden; she was safe from visitors in these retreats. She was so painfully shy she could not bear any special notice. One day, on being led in to dinner by a stranger, she trembled and nearly burst into tears; but notwithstanding her excessive shyness, which was often painful to others as well as herself, she won the respect and affection of all who had opportunity enough to become acquainted with her.

Charlotte's shyness did not arise, I am sure, either from vanity or self-consciousness, as some suppose shyness to arise; its source was (as Mr Arthur Helps says very truly in one of his recent essays) in her 'not being understood'. She felt herself apart from others; they did not *understand* her, and she keenly felt the distance.

A year later, Ellen Nussey visited Haworth. She provides us with a valuable glimpse of the characters of the other members of the Brontë family.

Emily Brontë had by this time acquired a lithesome, graceful figure. She was the tallest person in the house, except her father. Her hair, which was naturally as beautiful as Charlotte's, was in the same unbecoming tight curl and frizz, and there was the same want of complexion. She had very beautiful eyes – kind, kindling, liquid eyes; but she did not often look at you: she was too reserved. Their colour might be said to be dark grey, at other times dark blue, they varied so. She talked very little. She and Anne were like twins – inseparable companions, and in the very closest sympathy, which never had any interruption.

Anne – dear, gentle Anne – was quite different in appearance from the others. She was her aunt's favourite. Her hair was a very pretty, light brown, and fell on her neck in graceful curls. She had lovely violet-blue eyes, fine pencilled eyebrows, and clear, almost transparent complexion.

She still pursued her studies, and especially her sewing, under the surveillance of her aunt. Emily had now begun to have the disposal of her own time.

Branwell studied regularly with his father, and used to paint in oils, which was regarded as study for what might be eventually his profession. All the household entertained the idea of his becoming an artist, and hoped he would be a distinguished one.

In fine and suitable weather delightful rambles were made over the moors, and down into the glens and ravines that here and there broke the monotony of the moorland. The rugged bank and rippling brook were treasures of delight. Emily, Anne, and Branwell used to ford the streams, and sometimes placed stepping-stones for the other two; there was always a lingering delight in these spots – every moss, every flower, every tint and form, were noted and enjoyed. Emily especially had a gleesome delight in these nooks of beauty, – her reserve for the time vanished. One long ramble made in these early days was far away over the moors to a spot familiar to Emily and Anne, which they called 'The Meeting of the Waters'. It was a small oasis of emerald green turf, broken here and there by small clear springs; a few large stones served as resting-places; seated here, we were hidden from all the world, nothing appearing in view but miles and miles of heather, a glorious blue sky, and brightening sun. A fresh breeze wafted on us its exhilarating influence; we laughed and made mirth of each other, and settled we would call ourselves the quartette. Emily, half reclining on a slab of stone, played like a young child with the tadpoles in the water, making them swim about, and then fell to moralizing on the strong and the weak, the brave and the cowardly, as she chased them with her hand. No serious care or sorrow had so far cast its gloom on nature's youth and buoyancy, and nature's simplest offerings were fountains of pleasure and enjoyment.

The interior of the now far-famed parsonage lacked drapery of all kinds. Mr Brontë's horror of fire forbade curtains to the windows; they never had these accessories to comfort and appearance till long after Charlotte was the only inmate of the family sitting-room, – she then ventured on the innovation when her friend was with her; it did not please her father, but it was not forbidden.

There was not much carpet anywhere except in the sitting-room, and on the study floor. The hall floor and stairs were done with sand-stone, always beautifully clean, as everything was about the house; the walls were not papered, but stained in a pretty dove-coloured tint; hair-seated chairs and mahogany tables, book-shelves in the study, but not many of

Grasper – drawn by Emily

Pine Marten – watercolour by Charlotte

Flossie – painting by Charlotte

Right: Hero – painting by Emily

By E. J. C. B. to ⸻ Octr. 27th 1841.

these elsewhere. Scant and bare indeed, many will say, yet it was not a scantness that made itself felt. Mind and thought, I had almost said elegance, but certainly refinement, diffused themselves over all, and made nothing really wanting.

A little later on, there was the addition of a piano. Emily, after some application, played with precision and brilliancy. Anne played also, but she preferred soft harmonies and vocal music. She sang a little; her voice was weak, but very sweet in tone.

Mr Brontë's health caused him to retire early. He assembled his household for family worship at eight o'clock; at nine he locked and barred the front door, always giving as he passed the sitting-room door a kindly admonition to the 'children' not to be late; half-way up the stairs he stayed his steps to wind up the clock, the clock that in after days seemed to click like a dirge in the refrain of Longfellow's poem, 'The Old Clock on the Stairs':

'Forever – never!
Never – forever!'

Every morning was heard the firing of a pistol from Mr Brontë's room window, – it was the discharging of the loading which was made every night. Mr Brontë's tastes led him to delight in the perusal of battle-scenes, and in following the artifice of war; had he entered on military service instead of ecclesiastical he would probably have had a very distinguished career. The self-denials and privations of camp-life would have agreed entirely with his nature, for he was remarkably independent of the luxuries and comforts of life. The only dread he had was of *fire*, and this dread was so intense it caused him to prohibit all but silk or woollen dresses for his daughters; indeed, for any one to wear any other kind of fabric was almost to forfeit his respect.

Mr Brontë at times would relate strange stories, which had been told to him by some of the oldest inhabitants of the parish, of the extraordinary lives and doings of people who had resided in far-off, out-of-the-way places, but in contiguity with Haworth, – stories which made one shiver and shrink from hearing; but they were full of grim humour and interest to Mr Brontë and his children, as revealing the characteristics of a class in the human race, and as such Emily Brontë has stereotyped them in her *Wuthering Heights*.

*   *   *

In the middle of the summer of 1835 a great family plan was mooted at the parsonage. The question was, to what trade or profession should

Branwell be brought up? He was now nearly eighteen; it was time to decide. He was very clever, no doubt; perhaps, to begin with, the greatest genius in this rare family. The sisters hardly recognised their own or each other's powers, but they knew *his*. The father, ignorant of many failings in moral conduct, did proud homage to the great gifts of his son; for Branwell's talents were readily and willingly brought out for the entertainment of others. Popular admiration was sweet to him. And this led to his presence being sought at 'arvills' and all the great village gatherings, for the Yorkshiremen have a keen relish for intellect; and it likewise procured him the undesirable distinction of having his company recommended by the landlord of the 'Black Bull' to any chance traveller who might happen to feel solitary or dull over his liquor. 'Do you want some one to help you with your bottle, sir? If you do I'll send for Patrick' (so the villagers called him till the day of his death, though in his own family he was always 'Branwell'). And while the messenger went the landlord entertained his guest with accounts of the wonderful talents of the boy, whose precocious cleverness, and great conversational powers, were the pride of the village. The attacks of ill health to which Mr Brontë had been subject of late years rendered it not only necessary that he should take his dinner alone (for the sake of avoiding temptations to unwholesome diet), but made it also desirable that he should pass the time directly succeeding his meals in perfect quiet. And this necessity, combined with due attention to his parochial duties, made him partially ignorant how his son employed himself out of lesson time. His own youth had been spent among people of the same conventional rank as those into whose companionship Branwell was now thrown; but he had had a strong will, and an earnest and persevering ambition, and a resoluteness of purpose which his weaker son wanted.

Mrs Gaskell

In order to help finance Branwell's further education, Charlotte decided to take a position as a governess, as she announced in a letter to Ellen Nussey:

DEAR ELLEN, I had hoped to have had the extreme pleasure of seeing you at Haworth this summer, but human affairs are mutable, and human resolutions must bend to the course of events – We are all about to divide, break up, separate, Emily is going to school, Branwell is going to London, and I am going to be a Governess. This last determination I formed myself, knowing that I should have to take the step sometime, and 'better sune as syne' to use the Scotch proverb and knowing also that Papa would have enough to do with his limited income should Branwell be placed at the Royal Academy, and Emily at Roe-Head. Where am I going to reside? you will ask – within four miles of yourself dearest at a place neither of us are wholly unacquainted with, being no other than the identical Roe-Head mentioned above. Yes I am going to teach in the very school where I was myself taught – Miss Wooler made me the offer and I preferred it to one or two proposals of Private Governess-ship which I had before received – I am sad, very sad at the thoughts of leaving home but Duty – Necessity – these are stern mistresses who will not be disobeyed. Did I not once say Ellen you ought to be thankful for your independence? I felt what I said at the time, and I repeat it now with double earnestness: if any thing would cheer me, it is this idea of being so near you – surely you and Polly will come and see me – it would be wrong in me to doubt it – you were never unkind yet. Emily and I leave home on the 29th of this month, the idea of being together consoles us both somewhat, and in truth since I must enter a situation 'my lines have fallen in pleasant places' – I both love, and respect Miss Wooler. . . . remember me respectfully to Mrs Nussey, and believe me my dearest friend Affectionately, warmly Yours

C. Brontë

July 2nd, – 35

*   *   *

On July 29, 1835, Charlotte, now a little more than nineteen years old, went as teacher to Miss Wooler's. Emily accompanied her as a pupil; but she became literally ill from home-sickness, and could not settle to anything, and after passing only three months at Roe Head returned to the parsonage and the beloved moors.

Miss Brontë gives the following reasons as those which prevented Emily's remaining at school, and caused the substitution of her younger sister in her place at Miss Wooler's:–

'My sister Emily loved the moors. Flowers brighter than the rose bloomed in the blackest of the heath for her; out of a sullen hollow in a livid hillside her mind could make an Eden. She found in the bleak solitude many and dear delights; and not the least and best loved was – liberty. Liberty was the breath of Emily's nostrils; without it she perished. The change from her own home to a school, and from her own very noiseless, very secluded, but unrestricted and unartificial mode of life, to one of disciplined routine (though under the kindest auspices) was what she failed in enduring. Her nature proved here too strong for her fortitude. Every morning, when she woke, the vision of home and the moors rushed on her, and darkened and saddened the day that lay before her. Nobody knew what ailed her but me. I knew only too well. In this struggle her health was quickly broken: her white face, attenuated form, and failing strength threatened rapid decline. I felt in my heart she would die if she did not go home, and with this conviction obtained her recall. She had only been three months at school; and it was some years before the experiment of sending her from home was again ventured on.'

Mrs Gaskell

Charlotte's experiences at work were hardly any happier than Emily's. She was forced to leave Miss Wooler's school as a result of morbid depression but she was no happier as a private governess. She wrote to her sister, Emily, in June 1839:

I have striven hard to be pleased with my new situation. The country, the house, and the grounds are, as I have said, divine. But, alack-a-day! there is such a thing as seeing all beautiful around you – pleasant woods, winding white paths, green lawns, and blue sunshiny sky – and not having a free moment or a free thought left to enjoy them in. The children are constantly with me, and more riotous, perverse, unmanageable cubs never grew. As for correcting them, I soon quickly found that was entirely out of the question: they are to do as they like. A complaint to Mrs Sidgwick brings only black looks upon oneself, and unjust, partial excuses to screen the children. I have tried that plan once. It succeeded so notably that I shall try it no more. I said in my last letter that Mrs Sidgwick did not know me. I now begin to find that she does not intend to know me, that she cares nothing in the world about me except to contrive how the greatest possible quantity of labour may be squeezed out of me, and to that end she overwhelms me with oceans of needlework, yards of cambric to hem, muslin nightcaps to make, and, above all things, dolls to dress. I do not think she likes me at all, because I can't help being shy in such an entirely novel scene, surrounded as I have hitherto been by strange and constantly changing faces. I used to think I should like to be in the stir of grand folks' society but I have had enough of it – it is dreary work to look on and listen. I see now more clearly than I have ever done before that a private governess has no existence, is not considered as a living and rational being except as connected with the wearisome duties she has to fulfil. While she is teaching the children, working for them, amusing them, it is all right. If she steals a moment for herself she is a nuisance. Nevertheless, Mrs Sidgwick is universally considered an amiable woman. Her manners are fussily affable. She talks a great deal, but as it seems to me not much to the purpose. Perhaps I may like her better after a while. At present I have no call to like her. Mr Sidgwick is in my opinion a hundred times better – less profession, less bustling condescension, but a far kinder heart. It is very seldom that he speaks to me, but when he does I always feel happier and more settled for some minutes after. He never asks me to wipe the children's smutty noses or tie their shoes or fetch their pinafores or set them a chair. One of the pleasantest afternoons I have spent here – indeed, the only one at all pleasant – was when Mr Sidgwick walked out with his children, and I had orders to follow a little behind. As he strolled on through his fields with his magnificent Newfoundland dog at his side, he looked very like what a frank, wealthy, Conservative gentleman ought to be. He spoke freely and unaffectedly to the people he met, and though he indulged his children and allowed them to tease himself far too much, he would not suffer them grossly to insult others.

The other side of the situation is conveyed by a relative of Charlotte's employers:

Charlotte Brontë acted as governess to my cousins at Stonegappe for a few months in 1839. Few traditions of her connection with the Sidgwicks survive. She was, according to her own account, very unkindly treated, but it is clear that she had no gifts for the management of children, and was also in a very morbid condition the whole time. My cousin Benson Sidgwick, now vicar of Ashby Parva, certainly on one occasion threw a Bible at Miss Brontë! and all that another cousin can recollect of her is that if she was invited to walk to church with them, she thought she was being ordered about like a slave; if she was not invited, she imagined she was excluded from the family circle. Both Mr and Mrs John Sidgwick were extraordinarily benevolent people, much beloved, and would not wittingly have given pain to any one connected with them.

from *The Life of Edward White Benson* by A. C. Benson

A similar impression is also conveyed by an independent observer of Charlotte as governess in another family a couple of years later:

My mother, Mrs Slade of Hastings, now in her seventy-ninth year, distinctly remembers meeting the afterwards distinguished authoress at the house of Mr White, a Bradford merchant . . . something like sixty years ago. At that time Miss Brontë was acting as governess to Mrs

White's children, and my mother has a vivid recollection of seeing her sitting apart from the family in a corner of the room, poring, in her short-sighted way over a book. The impression she made on my mother was that of a shy, nervous girl, ill at ease, who desired to escape notice and to avoid taking part in the general conversation.

from a letter to *The Westminster Gazette*, May 1901
by Mrs Strickland of Halsteads, Hastings

Life was not, however, all work and in the summer of 1839, Charlotte and Ellen went for a holiday to Easton, near Bridlington. They stayed in the house of a farmer for one month and then went into lodgings for a week in Bridlington. Ellen Nussey left this account of the holiday, clearly the most enjoyable that Charlotte ever spent.

Charlotte's first visit to the sea-coast deserves a little more notice than her letters give of the circumstances – it was an event eagerly coveted, but hard to attain. Mr Brontë and Miss Branwell had all manners of doubts and fears and cautions to express, and Charlotte was sinking into despair – there seemed only one chance of securing her the pleasure; her friend must fetch her; this she did through the aid of a dear relative, who sent her to Haworth under safe convey, and in a carriage that would bring both Charlotte and her luggage – this step proved to be the very best thing possible, the surprise was so good in its effects, there was nothing to combat – everybody rose into high good humours, Branwell was grandiloquent, he declared 'it was a brave defeat, that the doubters were fairly taken aback'. You have only to *will* a thing to *get* it, so Charlotte's luggage was speedily prepared, and almost before the horse was rested there was a quiet but triumphant starting; the brother and sisters at home were not less happy than Charlotte herself in her now secured pleasure. It was the first of real freedom to be enjoyed either by herself or her friend, a first experience in railway travelling, which however, only conveyed them through half of the route, the stage-coach making the rest of the journey. Passengers being too numerous for this accommodation, Charlotte and her friend were sent on in an open 'Fly'; the weather was most delightful, the drive was enjoyed immensely, but they were unconsciously hastening on to a disappointment. Friends in the vicinity of the coast whither they were bound had been informed of their coming, and were ready to seize upon them; they met the coach, but it did not bring their expected young friends, and they had to depart, but not without leaving orders at the Hotel where the coach stopped for the capture of the occupants of the 'Fly'; a post-chaise was in readiness, in which they were to be driven off not to the bourne they were longing for (the seaside) but two or three miles away from it, here they were (though most unwilling) hospitably entertained and *detained* for a month. The day but one after their capture they walked to the sea, and as soon as they were near enough for Charlotte to see it in its expanse, she was quite overpowered, she could not speak till she had shed some tears – she signed to her friend to leave her and walk on; this she did for a few steps, knowing full well what Charlotte was passing through, and the stern efforts she was making to subdue her emotions – her friend turned to her as soon as she thought she might without inflicting pain; her eyes were red and swollen, she was still trembling, but submitted to be led onwards where the view was less impressive; for the remainder of the day she was very quiet, subdued, and exhausted. Distant glimpses of the German Ocean had been visible as the two friends neared the coast on the day of their arrival, but Charlotte being without her glasses, could not see them, and when they were described to her, she said, 'Don't tell me any more. Let me wait.' Whenever the sound of the sea reached her ears in the grounds around the house wherein she was a captive guest, her spirit longed to rush away and be close to it. At last their kind and generous entertainers yielded to their wishes and permitted them to take wing and go into lodgings for one week, but still protecting them by every-day visits, and bounteous provision from their dairy. What Charlotte and her friend had desired for themselves was, to be their own providers, believing in their inexperience that they could do great things with the small sum of money they each had at their disposal, but at the end of the week when bills were asked for, they were thoroughly enlightened as to the proprietors of the kind care which had guarded them – they discovered that moderate appetites and modest demands for attendance were of no avail as regarded the demands made upon their small finances. A week's experience sufficed to show them the wisdom of not prolonging their stay, though the realisation of enjoyment had been as intense as anticipation had depicted.

It is appropriate to glance aside, at this point, at Branwell's career. The 'cherished favourite' of the family was already giving cause for concern as this extract from Mrs Gaskell reveals.

The year 1840 found all the Brontës living at home, except Anne . . . for some reason with which I am unacquainted, the plan of sending Branwell to study at the Royal Academy had been relinquished; probably it was found, on inquiry, that the expenses of such a life were greater than his father's slender finances could afford, even with the help which Charlotte's labours at Miss Wooler's gave, by providing for Anne's board and education. I gather from what I have heard that Branwell must have been severely disappointed when the plan fell through. His talents were certainly very brilliant, and of this he was fully conscious, and fervently desired, by their use, either in writing or drawing, to make himself a name. At the same time he would probably have found his strong love of pleasure and irregular habits a great impediment in his path to fame; but these blemishes in his character were only additional reasons why he yearned after a London life, in which he imagined he could obtain every stimulant to his already vigorous intellect, while at the same time he would have a license of action to be found only in crowded cities. Thus his whole nature was attracted towards the metropolis; and many an hour must he have spent poring over the map of London, to judge from an anecdote which has been told me. Some traveller for a London house of business came to Haworth for a night, and, according to the unfortunate habit of the place, the brilliant 'Patrick' was sent for to the inn, to beguile the evening by his intellectual conversation and his flashes of wit. They began to talk of London; of the habits and ways of life there; of the places of amusement; and Branwell informed the Londoner of one or two short cuts from point to point, up narrow lanes or back streets; and it was only towards the end of the evening that the traveller discovered, from his companion's voluntary confession, that he had never set foot in London at all.

At this time the young man seemed to have his fate in his own hands. He was full of noble impulses, as well as of extraordinary gifts; not accustomed to resist temptation, it is true, from any higher motive than strong family affection, but showing so much power of attachment to all about him that they took pleasure in believing that, after a time, he would 'right himself', and that they should have pride and delight in the use he would then make of his splendid talents. His aunt especially made him her great favourite. There are always peculiar trials in the life of an only boy in a family of girls. He is expected to act a part in life; to *do*, while they are only to *be*; and the necessity of their giving way to him in some things is too often exaggerated into their giving way to him in all, and thus rendering him utterly selfish. In the family about whom I am writing, while the rest were almost ascetic in their habits, Branwell was allowed to grow up self-indulgent; but, in early youth, his power of attracting and attaching people was so great that few came in contact with him who were not so much dazzled by him as to be desirous of gratifying whatever wishes he expressed. Of course he was careful enough not to reveal anything before his father and sisters of the pleasures he indulged in; but his tone of thought and conversation became gradually coarser, and, for a time, his sisters tried to persuade themselves that such coarseness was a part of manliness, and to blind themselves by love to the fact that Branwell was worse than other young men. At present, though he had, they were aware, fallen into some errors, the exact nature of which they avoided knowing, still he was their hope and their darling; their pride, who should some time bring great glory to the name of Brontë.

He and his sister Charlotte were both slight and small of stature, while the other two were of taller and larger make. I have seen Branwell's profile; it is what would be generally esteemed very handsome; the forehead is massive, the eye well set, and the expression of it fine and intellectual; the nose too is good; but there are coarse lines about the mouth, and the lips, though of handsome shape, are loose and thick, indicating self-indulgence, while the slightly retreating chin conveys an idea of weakness of will. His hair and complexion were sandy. He had enough of Irish blood in him to make his manners frank and genial, with a kind of natural gallantry about them. In a fragment of one of his manuscripts which I have read there is a justness and felicity of expression which is very striking. It is the beginning of a tale, and the actors in it are drawn with much of the grace of characteristic portrait-painting, in perfectly pure and simple language which distinguishes so many of Addison's papers in the 'Spectator'. The fragment is too short to afford the means of judging whether he had much dramatic talent, as the persons of the story are not thrown into conversation. But altogether the elegance and composure of style are such as one would not have expected from this vehement and ill-fated young man. He had a stronger desire for literary fame burning in his heart than even that which occasionally flashed up in his sisters'. He tried various outlets for his talents. He wrote and sent poems to Wordsworth and Coleridge, who both expressed kind and laudatory opinions, and he frequently contributed verses to the 'Leeds Mercury'. In 1840 he was living at home, employing himself in occasional composition of various kinds, and waiting till some occupation, for which he might be fitted without any expensive course of preliminary training, should turn up; waiting, not impatiently; for he saw society of one kind (probably what he called 'life') at the 'Black Bull'; and at home he was as yet the cherished favourite.

Something of the coarsening to which Mrs Gaskell refers is
undoubtedly present in this letter from Branwell to John
Brown, sexton of Haworth and a drinking companion. It was
written from Broughton-in-Furness where Branwell was for
a short time employed as a tutor.

OLD KNAVE OF TRUMPS, Don't think I have forgotten you, though I have
delayed so long in writing to you. It was my purpose to send you a yarn as
soon as I could find materials to spin one with, and it is only just now that
I have had time to turn myself round and know where I am. If you saw me
now, you would not know me, and you would laugh to hear the character
the people give me. Oh, the falsehood and hypocrisy of this world! I am
fixed in a little retired town by the sea-shore, among wild, woody hills
that rise round me – huge, rocky, and capped with clouds. My employer
is a retired County magistrate, a large landowner, and of a right hearty
and generous disposition. His wife is a quiet, silent, and amiable woman,
and his sons are two fine, spirited lads. My landlord is a respectable
surgeon, two days out of seven is as drunk as a lord! His wife is a bustling,
chattering, kind-hearted soul; and his daughter! oh! death and
damnation! Well, what am I? That is, what do they think I am? A most
calm, sedate, sober, abstemious, patient, mild-hearted, virtuous,
gentlemanly philosopher, – the picture of good works, and the treasure-
house of righteous thoughts. Cards are shuffled under the table-cloth,
glasses are thrust into the cupboard if I enter the room. I take neither
spirits, wine, nor malt liquors. I dress in black, and smile like a saint or
martyr. Everybody says, 'what a good young gentleman is Mr
Postlethwaite's tutor!' This is a fact, as I am a living soul, and right
comfortably do I laugh at them. I mean to continue in their good opinion.
I took a half-year's farewell of old friend whisky at Kendal on the night
after I left. There was a party of gentlemen at the Royal Hotel, and I
joined them. We ordered in supper and whisky-toddy as 'hot as hell!'
They thought I was a physician, and put me in the chair. I gave sundry
toasts, that were washed down at the same time, till the room spun round
and the candles danced in our eyes. One of the guests was a respectable
old gentleman with powdered head, rosy cheeks, fat paunch, and ringed
fingers. He gave 'The Ladies', ... after which he brayed off with a
speech; and in two minutes, in the middle of a grand sentence, he
stopped, wiped his head, looked wildly round, stammered, coughed,
stopped again, and called for his slippers. The waiter helped him to bed.
Next a tall Irish squire and a native of the land of Israel began to quarrel

about their countries; and, in the warmth of argument, discharged their glasses, each at his neighbour's throat instead of his own. I recommended bleeding, purging, and blistering; but they administered each other a real 'Jem Warder', so I flung my tumbler on the floor, too, and swore I'd join 'Old Ireland!' A regular rumpus ensued, but we were tamed at last. I found myself in bed next morning, with a bottle of porter, a glass, and a corkscrew beside me. Since then I have not tasted anything stronger than milk-and-water, nor, I hope, shall, till I return at Midsummer; when we will see about it. I am getting as fat as Prince William at Springhead, and as godly as his friend, Parson Winterbotham. My hand shakes no longer. I ride to the banker's at Ulverston with Mr Postlethwaite, and sit drinking tea and talking scandal with old ladies. As to the young ones! I have one sitting by me just now – fair-faced, blue-eyed, dark-haired, sweet eighteen – she little thinks the devil is so near her!

During 1840 and 1841, a new project occupied the minds of the Brontë sisters. This was a plan to set up a small boarding school in the parsonage at Haworth. In this way they hoped to solve their financial problems and to keep the family together. Two strange diary entries written by Emily and Anne both refer to the school project and to their continued involvement in writing stories of Gondal, the Brontë imaginary land.

A PAPER to be opened
when Anne is
25 years old,
or my next birthday after
if
all be well.
Emily Jane Brontë. July the 30th, 1841

It is Friday evening, near 9 o'clock – wild rainy weather. I am seated in the dining-room alone, having just concluded tidying our desk boxes, writing this document. Papa is in the parlour – aunt upstairs in her room. She has been reading *Blackwood's Magazine* to papa. Victoria and Adelaide[1] are ensconced in the peat-house. Keeper is in the kitchen – Hero[2] in his cage. We are all stout and hearty, as I hope is the case with Charlotte, Branwell, and Anne, of whom the first is at John White, Esq., Upperwood House, Rawdon; the second is at Luddenden Foot; and the

[1] Two geese   [2] A hawk

The Misses Brontë's Establishment

FOR

THE BOARD AND EDUCATION

OF A LIMITED NUMBER OF

YOUNG LADIES,

THE PARSONAGE, HAWORTH,

NEAR BRADFORD.

Terms.

	£.	s.	d.
BOARD AND EDUCATION, including Writing, Arithmetic, History, Grammar, Geography, and Needle Work, per Annum, ...	35	0	0
French, .. German, .. Latin .. } each per Quarter, ...	1	1	0
Music, .. Drawing, .. } each per Quarter, ...	1	1	0
Use of Piano Forte, per Quarter, ...	0	5	0
Washing, per Quarter, ...	0	15	0

Each Young Lady to be provided with One Pair of Sheets, Pillow Cases, Four Towels, a Dessert and Tea-spoon.

A Quarter's Notice, or a Quarter's Board, is required previous to the Removal of a Pupil.

The prospectus for the proposed Brontë School. They received no applications so the project was abandoned third is, I believe, at Scarborough, inditing perhaps a paper corresponding to this.

A scheme is at present in agitation for setting us up in a school of our own; as yet nothing is determined, but I hope and trust it may go on and prosper and answer our highest expectations. This day four years I wonder whether we shall still be dragging on in our present condition or established to our hearts' content. Time will show.

I guess that at the time appointed for the opening of this paper we *i.e.* Charlotte, Anne, and I, shall be all merrily seated in our own sitting-room in some pleasant and flourishing seminary, having just gathered in for the midsummer holyday. Our debts will be paid off, and we shall have cash in hand to a considerable amount. Papa, aunt, and Branwell will either have been or be coming to visit us. It will be a fine warm summer evening, very different from this bleak look-out, and Anne and I will perchance slip out into the garden for a few minutes to peruse our papers. I hope either this or something better will be the case.

The *Gondalians* are at present in a threatening state, but there is no open rupture as yet. All the princes and princesses of the Royalty are at the Palace of Instruction. I have a good many books on hand, but I am sorry to say that as usual I make small progress with any. However, I have just made a new regularity paper! and I mean *verb sap* to do great things. And now I must close, sending from far an exhortation, 'Courage, courage', to exiled and harassed Anne, wishing she was here.

*   *   *

July the 30th, A.D. 1841

This is Emily's birthday. She has now completed her 23rd year, and is, I believe, at home. Charlotte is a governess in the family of Mr White. Branwell is a clerk in the railroad station at Luddenden Foot, and I am a governess in the family of Mr Robinson. I dislike the situation and wish to change it for another. I am now at Scarborough. My pupils are gone to bed and I am hastening to finish this before I follow them.

We are thinking of setting up a school of our own, but nothing definite is settled about it yet, and we do not know whether we shall be able to or not. I hope we shall. And I wonder what will be our condition and how or where we shall all be on this day four years hence; at which time, if all be well, I shall be 25 years and 6 months old, Emily will be 27 years old, Branwell 28 years and 1 month, and Charlotte 29 years and a quarter. We are now all separate and not likely to meet again for many a weary week, but we are none of us ill that I know of, and all are doing something for our own livelihood except Emily, who, however, is as busy as any of us, and in reality earns her food and raiment as much as we do.

How little know we what we are
How less what we may be!

Four years ago I was at school. Since then I have been a governess at Blake Hall, left it, come to Thorp Green, and seen the sea and York Minster. Emily has been a teacher at Miss Patchet's school, and left it. Charlotte has left Miss Wooler's, been a governess at Mrs Sidgwick's, left her, and gone to Mrs White's. Branwell has given up painting, been a tutor in Cumberland, left it, and become a clerk on the railroad. Tabby has left us, Martha Brown has come in her place. We have got Keeper, got a sweet little cat and lost it, and also got a hawk. Got a wild goose which has flown away, and three tame ones, one of which has been killed. All these diversities, with many others, are things we did not expect or foresee in the July of 1837. What will the next four years bring forth? Providence only knows. But we ourselves have sustained very little alteration since that time. I have the same faults that I had then, only I have more wisdom and experience, and a little more self-possession than I then enjoyed. How will it be when we open this paper and the one Emily has written? I wonder whether the *Gondalians* will still be flourishing, and what will be their condition. I am now engaged in writing the fourth volume of *Solala Vernon's Life*.

For some time I have looked upon 25 as a sort of era in my existence. It may prove a true presentiment, or it may be only a superstitious fancy; the latter seems most likely, but time will show.

Anne Brontë

3 Charlotte in Brussels and in love 1841–1845

The Brontë sisters' plan to establish a school persisted and by later in 1841 had taken a new turn, as this letter from Charlotte to her aunt, Miss Branwell, reveals.

UPPERWOOD HOUSE, RAWDON,
September 29th, 1841

DEAR AUNT, – I have heard nothing of Miss Wooler yet since I wrote to her intimating that I would accept her offer. I cannot conjecture the reason of this long silence, unless some unforeseen impediment has occurred in concluding the bargain. Meantime, a plan has been suggested and approved by Mr and Mrs White, and others, which I wish now to impart to you. My friends recommend me, if I desire to secure permanent success, to delay commencing the school for six months longer, and by all means to contrive, by hook or by crook, to spend the intervening time in some school on the Continent. They say schools in England are so numerous, competition so great, that without some such step towards attaining superiority we shall probably have a very hard struggle, and may fail in the end. They say, moreover, that the loan of £100, which you have been so kind as to offer us, will, perhaps, not be all required now, as Miss Wooler will lend us the furniture; and that, if the speculation is intended to be a good and successful one, half the sum, at least, ought to be laid out in the manner I have mentioned, thereby insuring a more speedy repayment both of interest and principal.

I would not go to France or to Paris. I would go to Brussels, in Belgium. The cost of the journey there, at the dearest rate of travelling, would be £5; living is there little more than half as dear as it is in England, and the facilities for education are equal or superior to any other place in Europe. In half a year, I could acquire a thorough familiarity with French. I could improve greatly in Italian, and even get a dash of German, *i.e.* providing my health continued as good as it is now. Martha

Taylor is now staying in Brussels, at a first-rate establishment there. I should not think of going to the Château de Kockleberg, where she is resident, as the terms are much too high; but if I wrote to her, she, with the assistance of Mrs Jenkins, the wife of the British Consul, would be able to secure me a cheap and decent residence and respectable protection. I should have the opportunity of seeing her frequently, she would make me acquainted with the city; and, with the assistance of her cousins, I should probably in time be introduced to connections far more improving, polished, and cultivated, than any I have yet known.

These are advantages which would turn to vast account, when we actually commenced a school – and, if Emily could share them with me, only for a single half-year, we could take a footing in the world afterwards which we can never do now. I say Emily instead of Anne; for Anne might take her turn at some future period, if our school answered. I feel certain, while I am writing, that you will see the propriety of what I say; you always like to use your money to the best advantage; you are not fond of making shabby purchases; when you do confer a favour, it is often done in style; and depend upon it £50, or £100, thus laid out, would be well employed. Of course, I know no other friend in the world to whom I could apply on this subject except yourself. I feel an absolute conviction that, if this advantage were allowed us, it would be the making of us for life. Papa will perhaps think it a wild and ambitious scheme; but who ever rose in the world without ambition? When he left Ireland to go to Cambridge University, he was as ambitious as I am now. I want us *all* to go on. I know we have talents, and I want them to be turned to account. I look to you, aunt, to help us. I think you will not refuse. I know, if you consent, it shall not be my fault if you ever repent your kindness. With love to all, and the hope that you are all well, – Believe me, dear aunt, your affectionate niece,

C. Brontë

Miss Branwell apparently agreed to the proposal for, in the spring of 1842, Charlotte and Emily went to Brussels. Charlotte's letters to Ellen Nussey reveal the pattern of their lives.

I was twenty-six years old a week or two since; and at this ripe time of life I am a schoolgirl, and, on the whole, very happy in that capacity. It felt very strange at first to submit to authority instead of exercising it – to obey orders instead of giving them; but I like that state of things. I returned to it with the same avidity that a cow, that has long been kept on dry hay, returns to fresh grass. Don't laugh at my simile. It is natural to me to submit, and very unnatural to command.

This is a large school, in which there are about forty *externes*, or day pupils, and twelve *pensionnaires*, or boarders. Madame Héger, the head, is a lady of precisely the same cast of mind, degree of cultivation, and quality of intellect as Miss (Catherine Wooler). I think the severe points are a little softened, because she has not been disappointed, and consequently soured. In a word, she is a married instead of a maiden lady. There are three teachers in the school – Mademoiselle Blanche, Mademoiselle Sophie, and Mademoiselle Marie. The two first have no particular character. One is an old maid, and the other will be one. Mademoiselle Marie is talented and original, but of repulsive and arbitrary manners, which have made the whole school, except myself and Emily, her bitter enemies. No less than seven masters attend, to teach the different branches of education—French, Drawing, Music, Singing, Writing, Arithmetic, and German. All in the house are Catholics except ourselves, one other girl, and the *gouvernante* of Madame's children, an Englishwoman, in rank something between a lady's maid and a nursery governess. The difference in country and religion makes a broad line of demarcation between us and all the rest. We are completely isolated in the midst of numbers. Yet I think I am never unhappy; my present life is so delightful, so congenial to my own nature, compared with that of a governess. My time, constantly occupied, passes too rapidly. Hitherto both Emily and I have had good health, and therefore we have been able to work well. There is one individual of whom I have not yet spoken – M. Héger, the husband of Madame. He is professor of rhetoric, a man of power as to mind, but very choleric and irritable in temperament. He is very angry with me just at present, because I have written a translation which he chose to stigmatise as '*peu correct*'. He did not tell me so, but wrote the word on the margin of my book, and asked, in brief, stern phrase, how it happened that my compositions were always better than my translations, adding that the thing seemed to him inexplicable. The fact is, some weeks ago, in a high-flown humour, he forbade me to use either dictionary or grammar in translating the most difficult English compositions into French. This makes the task rather arduous, and compels me every now and then to introduce an English word, which nearly plucks the eyes out of his head when he sees it. Emily and he don't draw well together at all. Emily works like a horse, and she has had great difficulties to contend with – far greater than I have had. Indeed, those who come to a French school for instruction ought previously to have

Le Pensionnat Héger, the school in Brussels attended by Emily and Charlotte and where Charlotte was later to become a teacher

acquired a considerable knowledge of the French language, otherwise they will lose a great deal of time, for the course of instruction is adapted to natives and not to foreigners; and in these large establishments they will not change their ordinary course for one or two strangers. The few private lessons that M: Héger has vouchsafed to give us are, I suppose, to be considered a great favour; and I can perceive they have already excited much spite and jealousy in the school.

You will abuse this letter for being short and dreary, and there are a hundred things which I want to tell you, but I have no time. Brussels is a beautiful city. The Belgians hate the English. Their external morality is more rigid than ours. To lace the stays without a handkerchief on the neck is considered a disgusting piece of indelicacy.

The sudden illness and death of Miss Branwell occasioned their return home in 1842 but towards the end of January in the

following year Charlotte returned alone to Brussels to take up a position as teacher in M. Héger's school.

Towards the end of January the time came for Charlotte to return to Brussels. Her journey thither was rather disastrous. She had to make her way alone; and the train from Leeds to London, which should have reached Euston Square early in the afternoon, was so much delayed that it did not get in till ten at night. She had intended to seek out the Chapter Coffee-house, where she had stayed before, and which would have been near the place where the steamboats lay; but she appears to have been frightened by the idea of arriving at an hour which, to Yorkshire notions, was so late and unseemly; and taking a cab, therefore, at the station, she drove straight to the London Bridge Wharf, and desired a waterman to row her to the Ostend packet, which was to sail the next morning. She described to me, pretty much as she has since described it in 'Villette', her sense of loneliness, and yet her strange pleasure in the excitement of the situation, as in the dead of that winter's night she went swiftly over the dark river to the black hull's side, and was at first refused leave to ascend to the deck. 'No passengers might sleep on board,' they said, with some appearance of disrespect. She looked back to the lights and subdued noises of London – that 'Mighty Heart' in which she had no place – and, standing up in the rocking boat, she asked to speak to some one in authority on board the packet. He came, and her quiet, simple statement of her wish, and her reason for it, quelled the feeling of sneering distrust in those who had first heard her request; and impressed the authority so favourably that he allowed her to come on board, and take possession of a berth. The next morning she sailed; and at seven on Sunday evening she reached the Rue d'Isabelle once more, having only left Haworth on Friday morning at an early hour.

  Her salary was 16*l*. a year; out of which she had to pay for her German lessons, for which she was charged as much (the lessons being probably rated by time) as when Emily learnt with her and divided the expense, viz. ten francs a month. By Miss Brontë's own desire she gave her English lessons in the *classe*, or schoolroom, without the supervision of Madame or M. Héger. They offered to be present, with a view to maintain order among the unruly Belgian girls; but she declined this, saying that she would rather enforce discipline by her own manner and character than be indebted for obedience to the presence of a *gendarme*. She ruled over a new schoolroom, which had been built on the space in the playground adjoining the house. Over that First Class she was *surveillante* at all hours; and henceforward she was called *Mademoiselle* Charlotte by M. Héger's orders. She continued her own studies, principally attending to German and to Literature; and every Sunday she went alone to the German and English chapels. Her walks too were solitary, and principally taken in the *allée défendue*, where she was secure from intrusion. This solitude was a perilous luxury to one of her temperament, so liable as she was to morbid and acute mental suffering.

Mrs Gaskell

Charlotte's letter to Emily of May 29th 1843 shows that she is only too well aware of her isolation in the school.

. . . I am richly off for companionship in these parts. Of late days, M. and Mme Héger rarely speak to me, and I really don't pretend to care a fig for any body else in the establishment. You are not to suppose by that expression that I am under the influence of *warm* affection for Mme Héger. I am convinced that she does not like me – why, I can't tell, nor do I think she herself has any definite reason for the aversion; but for one thing, she cannot comprehend why I do not make intimate friends of Mesdames Blanche, Sophie, and Haussé. M. Héger is wondrously influenced by Madame, and I should not wonder if he disapproves very much of my unamiable want of sociability. He has already given me a brief lecture on universal *bienveillance*, and, perceiving that I don't improve in consequence, I fancy he has taken to considering me as a person to be let alone – left to the error of her ways; and consequently he has in a great measure withdrawn the light of his countenance, and I get on from day to day in a Robinson-Crusoe-like condition – very lonely. That does not signify. In other respects I have nothing substantial to complain of, nor is even this a cause for complaint. Except the loss of M. Héger's goodwill (if I have lost it) I care for none of 'em. I hope you are well and hearty. Walk out often on the moors. . . .

By September of the same year the isolation was almost more than Charlotte could bear. During the summer months the school was empty and Charlotte was almost entirely alone for weeks. She records in this letter to Emily a remarkable exploit for one of such firm Protestant conviction.

BRUSSELS, September 2nd, 1843

DEAR E. J., – Another opportunity of writing to you coming to pass, I shall improve it by scribbling a few lines. More than half the holidays are now past, and rather better than I expected. The weather has been exceedingly fine during the last fortnight, and yet not so Asiatically hot as it was last year at this time. Consequently I have tramped about a great deal and tried to get a clearer acquaintance with the streets of Brussels. This week, as no teacher is here except Mlle Blanche, who is returned from Paris, I am always alone except at meal-times, for Mlle Blanche's character is so false and so contemptible I can't force myself to associate with her. She perceives my utter dislike and never now speaks to me – a great relief.

However, I should inevitably fall into the gulf of low spirits if I stayed always by myself here without a human being to speak to, so I go out and traverse the Boulevards and streets of Brussels sometimes for hours together. Yesterday I went on a pilgrimage to the cemetery, and far beyond it on to a hill where there was nothing but fields as far as the horizon. When I came back it was evening; but I had such a repugnance to return to the house, which contained nothing that I cared for, I still kept threading the streets in the neighbourhood of the Rue d'Isabelle and avoiding it. I found myself opposite to Ste Gudule, and the bell, whose voice you know, began to toll for evening *salut*. I went in, quite alone (which procedure you will say is not much like me), wandered about the aisles where a few old women were saying their prayers, till vespers began. I stayed till they were over. Still I could not leave the church or force myself to go home – to school I mean. An odd whim came into my head. In a solitary part of the Cathedral six or seven people still remained kneeling by the confessionals. In two confessionals I saw a priest. I felt as if I did not care what I did, provided it was not absolutely wrong, and that it served to vary my life and yield a moment's interest. I took a fancy to change myself into a Catholic and go and make a real confession to see what it was like. Knowing me as you do, you will think this odd, but when people are by themselves they have singular fancies. A penitent was occupied in confessing. They do not go into the sort of pew or cloister which the priest occupies, but kneel down on the steps and confess through a grating. Both the confessor and the penitent whisper very low, you can hardly hear their voices. After I had watched two or three penitents go and return, I approached at last and knelt down in a niche which was just vacated. I had to kneel there ten minutes waiting, for on the other side was another penitent invisible to me. At last that went away and a little wooden door inside the grating opened, and I saw the priest leaning his ear towards me. I was obliged to begin, and yet I did not know a word of the formula with which they always commence their confessions. It was a funny position. I felt precisely as I did when alone on the Thames at midnight. I commenced with saying I was a foreigner and had been brought up a Protestant. The priest asked if I was a Protestant then. I somehow could not tell a lie, and said 'yes'. He replied that in that case I could not '*jouir du bonheur de la confesse*'; but I was determined to confess, and at last he said he would allow me because it might be the first step towards returning to the true church. I actually did confess – a real confession. When I had done he told me his address, and said that every morning I was to go to the Rue du Parc – to his house – and he would reason with me and try to convince me of the error and enormity of being a Protestant!!! I promised faithfully to go. Of course, however, the adventure stops there, and I hope I shall never see the priest again. I think you had better not tell papa of this. He will not understand that it was only a freak, and will perhaps think I am going to turn Catholic. Trusting that you and papa are well, and also Tabby and the Hoyles, and hoping you will write to me immediately, – I am, yours,

C. B.

In her novel, *Villette*, Charlotte gives a more intense account of the same experience:

One evening – and I was not delirious: I was in my sane mind, I got up – I dressed myself, weak and shaking. The solitude and the stillness of the long dormitory could not be borne any longer; the ghastly white beds were turning into spectres – the coronal of each became a death's-head, huge and sun-bleached – dead dreams of an elder world and mightier race lay frozen in their wide gaping eyeholes. That evening more firmly than ever fastened into my soul the conviction that Fate was of stone, and Hope a false idol – blind, bloodless, and of granite core. I felt, too, that the trial God had appointed me was gaining its climax, and must now be turned by my own hands, hot, feeble, trembling as they were. It rained still, and blew; but with more clemency, I thought, than it had poured and raged all day. Twilight was falling, and I deemed its influence pitiful; from the lattice I saw coming night-clouds trailing low like banners drooping. It seemed to me that at this hour there was affection and sorrow in Heaven above for all pain suffered on earth beneath; the weight of my dreadful dream became alleviated – that insufferable thought of being no more loved – no more owned, half-yielded to hope of the contrary – I was sure this hope would shine clearer if I got out from under this house-roof, which was crushing as the slab of a tomb, and went outside the city to a certain quiet hill, a long way distant in the fields. Covered with a cloak (I could not be delirious, for I had sense and recollection to put on warm clothing), forth I set. The bells of a church arrested me in passing; they seemed to call me in to the *salut*, and I went in. Any solemn rite, any spectacle of sincere worship, any opening for appeal to God was as welcome to me then as bread to one in extremity of want. I knelt down with others on the stone pavement. It was an old solemn church, its pervading gloom not gilded but purpled by light shed through stained glass.

Few worshippers were assembled, and, the *salut* over, half of them departed. I discovered soon that those left remained to confess. I did not stir. Carefully every door of the church was shut; a holy quiet sank upon, and a solemn shade gathered about us. After a space, breathless and spent in prayer, a penitent approached the confessional. I watched. She whispered her avowal; her shrift was whispered back; she returned consoled. Another went, and another. A pale lady, kneeling near me, said in a low, kind voice:– 'Go you now, I am not quite prepared.'

Mechanically obedient, I rose and went. I knew what I was about; my mind had run over the intent with lightning-speed. To take this step could not make me more wretched than I was; it might soothe me.

The priest within the confessional never turned his eyes to regard me; he only quietly inclined his ear to my lips. He might be a good man, but this duty had become to him a sort of form: he went through it with the phlegm of custom. I hesitated; of the formula of confession I was ignorant: instead of commencing, then, with the prelude usual, I said:– 'Mon père, je suis Protestante.'

He directly turned. He was not a native priest: of that class, the cast of physiognomy is, almost invariably, grovelling: I saw by his profile and brow he was a Frenchman; though grey and advanced in years, he did not, I think, lack feeling or intelligence. He inquired, not unkindly, why, being a Protestant, I came to him?

I said I was perishing for a word of advice or an accent of comfort. I had been living for some weeks quite alone; I had been ill; I had a pressure of affliction on my mind of which it would hardly any longer endure the weight.

'Was it a sin, a crime?' he inquired, somewhat startled.

I reassured him on this point, and, as well as I could, I showed him the mere outline of my experience.

He looked thoughtful, surprised, puzzled. 'You take me unawares,' said he. 'I have not had such a case as yours before: ordinarily we know our routine, and are prepared; but this makes a great break in the common course of confession. I am hardly furnished with counsel fitting the circumstances.'

Of course, I had not expected he would be; but the mere relief of communication in an ear which was human and sentient, yet consecrated – the mere pouring out of some portion of long accumulating, long pent-up pain into a vessel whence it could not be again diffused – had done me good. I was already solaced.

'Must I go, father?' I asked of him as he sat silent.

'My daughter,' he said kindly – and I am sure he was a kind man: he had a compassionate eye – 'for the present you had better go: but I assure you your words have struck me. Confession, like other things, is apt to become formal and trivial with habit. You have come and poured your heart out; a thing seldom done. I would fain think your case over, and take it with me to my oratory. Were you of our faith I should know what to say – a mind so tossed can find repose but in the bosom of retreat, and the punctual practice of piety. The world, it is well known, has no satisfaction for that class of natures. Holy men have bidden penitents like you to hasten their path upward by penance, self-denial, and difficult good works. Tears are given them here for meat and drink – bread of affliction and waters of affliction – their recompense comes hereafter. It is my own conviction that these impressions under which you are smarting are messengers from God to bring you back to the true Church. You were made for our faith: depend upon it our faith alone could heal and help you – Protestantism is altogether too dry, cold, prosaic for you. The further I look into this matter, the more plainly I see it is entirely out of the common order of things. On no account would I lose sight of you. Go, my daughter, for the present; but return to me again.'

I rose and thanked him. I was withdrawing when he signed me to return.

'You must not come to this church,' said he: 'I see you are ill, and this church is too cold; you must come to my house: I live——' (and he gave me his address). 'Be there to-morrow morning at ten.'

In reply to this appointment, I only bowed; and pulling down my veil, and gathering round me my cloak, I glided away.

Did I, do you suppose, reader, contemplate venturing again within that worthy priest's reach? As soon should I have thought of walking into a Babylonish furnace. That priest had arms which could influence me: he was naturally kind, with a sentimental French kindness, to whose softness I knew myself not wholly impervious. Without respecting some sorts of affection, there was hardly any sort having a fibre of root in reality, which I could rely on my force wholly to withstand. Had I gone to him, he would have shown me all that was tender, and comforting, and gentle, in the honest Popish superstition. Then he would have tried to kindle, blow and stir up in me the zeal of good works. I know not how it would all have ended. We all think ourselves strong in some points; we all know ourselves weak in many; the probabilities are that had I visited Numéro 10, Rue des Mages, at the hour and day appointed, I might just now, instead of writing this heretic narrative, be counting my beads in the cell of a certain Carmelite convent on the Boulevard of Crécy, in Villette. There was something of Fénelon about that benign old priest, and whatever most of his brethren may be, and whatever I may think of his Church and creed (and I like neither), of himself I must ever retain a grateful recollection. He was kind when I needed kindness; he did me good. May Heaven bless him!

Charlotte stayed in Brussels until the end of 1843. Her stay there was an intense experience which made a deep impression upon her and out of it grew her last, and perhaps her finest, novel, *Villette*. Lucy Snowe, the heroine of that novel, becomes passionately attached to a fiery little teacher in the school whose character is clearly based on that of M. Héger. We cannot doubt that Charlotte's feelings had been aroused to an equal intensity when we read the letters she wrote to M. Héger after she had returned to England. The letters are printed here in translation from the original French.

January 8th, 1845

Mr Taylor has returned. I asked him if he had a letter for me. 'No; nothing.' 'Patience,' said I – 'his sister will be here soon.' Miss Taylor has returned. 'I have nothing for you from Monsieur Héger,' says she; 'neither letter nor message.'

Having realized the meaning of these words, I said to myself what I should say to another similarly placed: 'You must be resigned, and above all do not grieve at a misfortune which you have not deserved.' I strove to restrain my tears, to utter no complaint.

But when one does not complain, when one seeks to dominate oneself with a tyrant's grip, the faculties start into rebellion, and one pays for external calm with an internal struggle that is almost unbearable.

Day and night I find neither rest nor peace. If I sleep I am disturbed by tormenting dreams in which I see you, always severe, always grave, always incensed against me.

Forgive me then, Monsieur, if I adopt the course of writing to you again. How can I endure life if I make no effort to ease its sufferings?

I know that you will be irritated when you read this letter. You will say once more that I am hysterical [or neurotic] – that I have black thoughts, &c. So be it, Monsieur; I do not seek to justify myself; I submit to every sort of reproach. All I know is that I cannot, that I will not, resign myself to lose wholly the friendship of my master. I would rather suffer the greatest physical pain than always have my heart lacerated by smarting regrets.

If my master withdraws his friendship from me entirely I shall be altogether without hope; if he gives me a little – just a little – I shall be satisfied – happy; I shall have reason for living on, for working.

Monsieur, the poor have not need of much to sustain them – they ask only for the crumbs that fall from the rich men's table. But if they are refused the crumbs they die of hunger. Nor do I, either, need much affection from those I love. I should not know what to do with a friendship entire and complete – I am not used to it. But you showed me of yore a *little* interest, when I was your pupil in Brussels, and I hold on to the maintenance of that *little* interest – I hold on to it as I would hold on to life.

You will tell me perhaps – 'I take not the slightest interest in you, Mademoiselle Charlotte. You are no longer an inmate of my House; I have forgotten you.'

Well, Monsieur, tell me so frankly. It will be a shock to me. It matters not. It would be less dreadful than uncertainty.

I shall not re-read this letter. I send it as I have written it. Nevertheless, I have a hidden consciousness that some people, cold and commonsense, in reading it would say – 'She is talking nonsense.' I would avenge myself on such persons in no other way than by wishing them one single day of the torments which I have suffered for eight months. We should then see if they would not talk nonsense too.

One suffers in silence so long as one has the strength so to do, and when that strength gives out one speaks without too carefully measuring one's words.

I wish Monsieur happiness and prosperity.

C. B.

That letter was written a year after Charlotte had finally left Brussels. Ten months later she wrote her last letter to M. Héger.

November 18th, 1845

MONSIEUR, – The six months of silence have run their course. It is now the 18th of Novr.; my last letter was dated (I think) the 18th of May. I may therefore write to you without failing in my promise.

The summer and autumn seemed very long to me; truth to tell, it has needed painful efforts on my part to bear hitherto the self-denial which I have imposed on myself. You, Monsieur, you cannot conceive what it means; but suppose for a moment that one of your children was separated from you, 160 leagues away, and that you had to remain six months without writing to him, without receiving news of him, without hearing him spoken of, without knowing aught of his health, then you would understand easily all the harshness of such an obligation. I tell you frankly that I have tried meanwhile to forget you, for the remembrance of a person whom one thinks never to see again, and whom, nevertheless, one greatly esteems, frets too much the mind; and when one has suffered that kind of anxiety for a year or two, one is ready to do anything to find peace once more. I have done everything; I have sought occupations; I have denied myself absolutely the pleasure of speaking about you – even to Emily; but I have been able to conquer neither my regrets nor my impatience. That, indeed, is humiliating – to be unable to control one's own thoughts, to be the slave of a regret, of a memory, the slave of a fixed and dominant idea which lords it over the mind. Why cannot I have just as much friendship for you, as you for me – neither more nor less? Then should I be so tranquil, so free – I could keep silence then for ten years without an effort.

My father is well but his sight is almost gone. He can neither read nor write. Yet the doctors advise waiting a few months more before attempting an operation. The winter will be a long night for him. He rarely complains; I admire his patience. If Providence wills the same calamity for me, may He at least vouchsafe me as much patience with which to bear it! It seems to me, Monsieur, that there is nothing more galling in great physical misfortunes than to be compelled to make all those about us share in our sufferings. The ills of the soul one can hide, but those which attack the body and destroy the faculties cannot be concealed. My father allows me now to read to him and write for him; he shows me, too, more confidence than he has ever shown before, and that is a great consolation.

Monsieur, I have a favour to ask of you: when you reply to this letter, speak to me a little of yourself, not of me; for I know that if you speak of me it will be to scold me, and this time I would see your kindly side. Speak to me therefore of your children. Never was your brow severe when Louise and Claire and Prosper were by your side. Tell me also something of the School, of the pupils, of the Governesses. Are Mesdemoiselles Blanche, Sophie, and Justine still at Brussels? Tell me where you travelled during the holidays – did you go to the Rhine? Did you not visit Cologne or Coblentz? Tell me, in short, my master, what you will, but tell me something. To write to an ex-assistant-governess (No! I refuse to remember my employment as assistant-governess – I repudiate it) – anyhow, to write to an old pupil cannot be a very interesting occupation for you, I know; but for me it is life. Your last letter was stay and prop to me – nourishment to me for half a year. Now I need another and you will give it me; not because you bear me friendship – you cannot have much – but because you are compassionate of soul and you would condemn no one to prolonged suffering to save yourself a few moments' trouble. To forbid me to write to you, to refuse to answer me, would be to tear from me my only joy on earth, to deprive me of my last privilege – a privilege I never shall consent willingly to surrender. Believe me, my master, in writing to me it is a good deed that you will do. So long as I believe you are pleased with me, so long as I have hope of receiving news from you, I can be at rest and not too sad. But when a prolonged and gloomy silence seems to threaten me with the estrangement of my master – when day by day I await a letter, and when day by day disappointment comes to fling me back into overwhelming sorrow, and the sweet delight of seeing your handwriting and reading your counsel escapes me as a vision that is vain, then fever claims me – I lose appetite and sleep – I pine away.

May I write to you again next May? I would rather wait a year, but it is impossible – it is too long.

C. Brontë

4 Branwell's decline and death 1845–1848

Charlotte's deeply passionate attachment to M. Héger was not the only cause of intense distress in the years following her return from Brussels. The decline of Branwell had begun. He gives his own reasons for his descent into apathy and hopelessness in the following letter to Francis H. Grundy:

October 1845

Since I last shook hands with you in Halifax, two summers ago, my life till lately has been one of apparent happiness and indulgence. You will ask, 'Why does he complain then?' I can only reply by showing the under-current of distress which bore my bark to a whirlpool, despite the surface waves of life that seemed floating me to peace. In a letter begun in the spring and never finished, owing to incessant attacks of illness, I tried to tell you that I was tutor to the son of [Mr Edmund Robinson, Thorp Green Hall], a wealthy gentleman whose wife is sister to the wife of ——, M.P., for the county of ——, and the cousin of Lord ——. This lady (though her husband detested me) showed me a degree of kindness which, when I was deeply grieved one day at her husband's conduct, ripened into declarations of more than ordinary feeling. My admiration of her mental and personal attractions, my knowledge of her unselfish sincerity, her sweet temper, and unwearied care for others, with but unrequited return where most should have been given . . . although she is seventeen years my senior, all combined to an attachment on my part, and led to reciprocations which I had little looked for. During nearly three years I had daily 'troubled pleasure soon chastised by fear'. Three months since, I received a furious letter from my employer, threatening to shoot me if I returned from my vacation, which I was passing at home; and letters from her lady's-maid and physician informed me of the outbreak, only checked by her firm courage and resolution that whatever harm came to her, none should come to me . . . I have lain during nine

A silhouette of Branwell Brontë

long weeks utterly shattered in body and broken down in mind. The probability of her becoming free to give me herself and estate never rose to drive away the prospect of her decline under her present grief. I dreaded, too, the wreck of my mind and body, which, God knows during a short life have been severely tried. Eleven continuous nights of sleepless horror reduced me to almost blindness, and being taken into Wales to recover, the sweet scenery, the sea, the sound of music caused me fits of unspeakable distress. You will say, 'What a fool!' but if you knew the many causes I have for sorrow which I cannot even hint at here, you would perhaps pity as well as blame. At the kind request of Mr Macaulay and Mr Baines, I have striven to arouse my mind by writing something worthy of being read, but I really cannot do so. Of course, you will despise the writer of all this. I can only answer that the writer does the same, and would not wish to live if he did not hope that work and change may yet restore him.

Apologizing sincerely for what seems like whining egotism, and hardly daring to hint about days when in your company I could sometimes sink the thoughts which 'remind me of departed days', I fear departed never to return, I remain, etc.

P. B. Brontë

Sketches drawn by Branwell in the year of his death.
Above a morbid view of a head in a noose which is
thought to be a self-portrait; below a drinking scene

Branwell's drawing of Mrs Robinson, mistress of Thorp Green

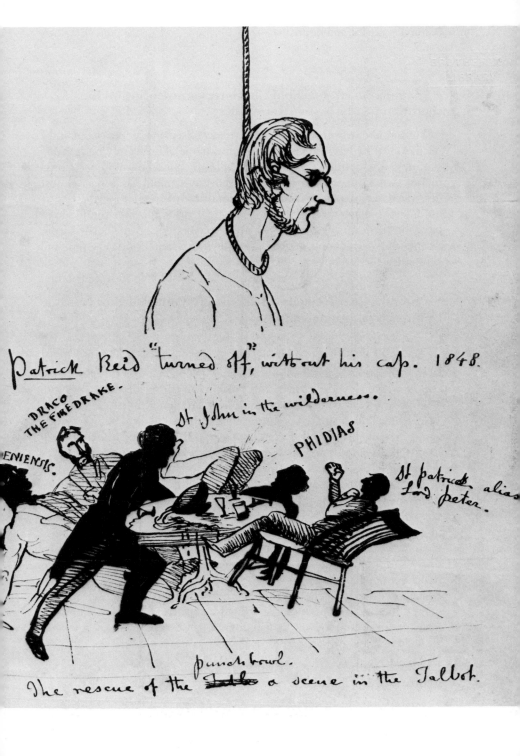

Patrick Reid "turned off" without his cap. 1848.

DRACO THE FIREDRAKE.

St John in the wilderness.

...ENIENSIS.

PHIDIAS

St patrick alias Lord peter.

punch bowl.

The rescue of the ~~Idols~~ a scene in the Talbot.

A few months later we find Charlotte commenting on his condition in a letter to Miss Wooler:

You ask about Branwell; he never thinks of seeking employment and I begin to fear he has rendered himself incapable of filling any respectable station in life, besides, if money were at his disposal he would use it only to his own injury – the faculty of self-government is, I fear almost destroyed in him – You ask me if I do not think men are strange beings – I do indeed, I have often thought so – and I think too that the mode of bringing them up is strange, they are not half sufficiently guarded from temptation – girls are protected as if they were something very frail and silly indeed while boys are turned loose on the world as if they – of all beings in existence, were the wisest and the least liable to be led astray.

Six months later she tells Ellen Nussey about a further crisis in Branwell's emotional state:

June 17th, '46

. . . We, I am sorry to say, have been somewhat more harassed than usual lately. The death of Mr Robinson, which took place about three weeks or a month ago, served Branwell for a pretext to throw all about him into hubbub and confusion with his emotions, etc., etc. Shortly after, came news from all hands that Mr Robinson had altered his will before he died and effectually prevented all chance of a marriage between his widow and Branwell, by stipulating that she should not have a shilling if she ever ventured to reopen any communication with him. Of course, he then became intolerable. To papa he allows rest neither day nor night, and he is continually screwing money out of him, sometimes threatening that he will kill himself if it is withheld from him. He says Mrs Robinson is now insane; that her mind is a complete wreck owing to remorse for her conduct towards Mr Robinson (whose end it appears was hastened by distress of mind) and grief for having lost him. I do not know how much to believe of what he says, but I fear she is very ill. Branwell declares that he neither can nor will do anything for himself; good situations have been offered him more than once, for which, by a fortnight's work, he might have qualified himself, but he will do nothing, except drink and make us all wretched.

By the beginning of 1847 Branwell was in an even more neurotic state, as this letter to J. B. Leyland shows:

I had reason to hope that ere very long I should be the husband of a

1844.

Thorp Green drawn by Branwell. Anne and Branwell were employed here as governess and tutor by the Rev and Mrs Robinson.

Lady whom I loved best in the world, and with whom, in more than competence, I might live at leisure to try to make myself a name in the world of posterity, without being pestered by the small but countless botherments, which like mosquitoes sting us in the world of work–day toil. That hope, and herself are *gone – She* to wither into patiently pining decline – *It* to make room for drudgery falling on one now ill fitted to bear it.

That ill-fittedness rises from causes which I should find myself able partially to overcome had I bodily strength, but with the want of that, and with the presence of daily lacerated nerves the task is not easy. I have been in truth too much petted through life, and in my last situation I was so much master, and gave myself so much up to enjoyment, that now when the cloud of ill-health and adversity has come upon me it will be a disheartning job to work myself up again through a new life's battle, from the position of five years ago to which I have been compelled to retreat with heavy loss and no gain. My army stands now where it did then, but mourning the slaughter of Youth, Health, Hope, and both mental and physical elasticity.

... I used to think that if I could have for a week the free range of the British Museum – the Library included – I could feel as though I were placed for seven days in Paradise, but now, really, dear sir, my eyes would roam over the Elgin marbles, the Egyptian saloon and the most treasured volumes like the eyes of a dead cod fish.

My rude rough aquaintances here ascribe my unhappiness solely to causes produced by my sometimes irregular life, because they have known no other pains than those resulting from excess or want of ready cash. They do not know that I would rather want a shirt than want a springy mind, and that my total want of happiness, were I to step into York Minster now, would be far, far worse than their want of an hundred pounds when they might happen to need it, and that if a dozen glasses or a bottle of wine drives off their cares, such cures only make me outwardly passable in company but *never* drive off mine.

I know only that it is time for me to be something when I am nothing. That my father cannot have long to live, and that when he dies, my evening, which is already twilight, will become night – That I shall then have a constitution still so strong that it will keep me years in torture and despair when I should every hour pray that I might die.

For the last three years of Branwell's life he took opium habitually, by way of stunning conscience; he drank, moreover, whenever he could get the opportunity. The reader may say that I have mentioned his tendency to intemperance long before. It is true; but it did not become habitual, as far as I can learn, until after he was dismissed from his tutorship. He took opium, because it made him forget for a time more effectually than drink; and, besides, it was more portable. In procuring it he showed all the cunning of the opium-eater. He would steal out while the family were at church – to which he had professed himself too ill to go – and manage to cajole the village druggist out of a lump; or, it might be, the carrier had unsuspiciously brought him some in a packet from a distance. For some time before his death he had attacks of delirium tremens of the most frightful character; he slept in his father's room, and he would sometimes declare that either he or his father would be dead before the morning. The trembling sisters, sick with fright, would implore their father not to expose himself to this danger; but Mr Brontë is no timid man, and perhaps he felt that he could possibly influence his son to some self-restraint, more by showing trust in him than by showing fear. The sisters often listened for the report of a pistol in the dead of the night, till watchful eye and hearkening ear grew heavy and dull with the perpetual strain upon their nerves. In the mornings young Brontë would saunter out, saying, with a drunkard's incontinence of speech, 'The poor old man and I have had a terrible night of it; he does his best – the poor old man! but it's all over with me.'

Mrs Gaskell

Branwell died in September 1848. A sad note to John Brown shows the depths to which he sank a few months before his death. It is followed by Francis Grundy's account of his last meeting with him.

Sunday, Noon

DEAR JOHN, – I shall feel very much obliged to you if [you] can contrive to get me Five pence worth of Gin in a proper measure.

Should it be speedily got I could perhaps take it from you or Billy at the lane top, or, what would be quite as well, sent out for, to you.

I anxiously ask the favour because I know the good it will do me.

Punctually at Half-past Nine in the morning you will be paid the 5d out of a shilling given me then. – Yours,

P.B.B.

As he never came to see me, I shortly made up my mind to visit him at Haworth, and was shocked at the wrecked and wretched appearance he

Branwell's painting of his friend John Brown

presented. Yet he still craved for an appointment of any kind, in order that he might try the excitement of change; of course uselessly. . . . Very soon I went to Haworth again to see him, for the last time. From the little inn I sent for him to the great, square, cold-looking Rectory. I had ordered a dinner for two, and the room looked cosy and warm, the bright glass and silver pleasantly reflecting the sparkling firelight, deeply toned by the red curtains. Whilst I waited his appearance, his father was shown in. Much of the Rector's old stiffness of manner was gone. He spoke of Branwell with more affection than I had ever heretofore heard him express, but he also spoke almost hopelessly. He said that when my message came, Branwell was in bed, and had been almost too weak for the last few days to leave it; nevertheless, he had insisted upon coming, and would be there immediately. We parted, and I never saw him again.

Presently the door opened cautiously, and a head appeared. It was a mass of red, unkempt, uncut hair, wildly floating round a great, gaunt forehead; the cheeks yellow and hollow, the mouth fallen, the thin white lips not trembling but shaking, the sunken eyes, once small, now glaring with the light of madness, – all told the sad tale but too surely. I hastened to my friend, greeted him in my gayest manner, as I knew he best liked, drew him quickly into the room, and forced upon him a stiff glass of hot brandy. Under its influence, and that of the bright, cheerful surroundings, he looked frightened – frightened of himself. He glanced at me for a moment, and muttered something of leaving a warm bed to come out into the cold night. Another glass of brandy, and returning warmth gradually brought him back to something like the Brontë of old. He even ate some dinner, a thing which he said he had not done for long; so our last interview was pleasant, though grave. I never knew his intellect clearer. He described himself as waiting anxiously for death – indeed, longing for it, and happy, in these his sane moments, to think that it was so near. He once again declared that that death would be due to the story I knew, and to nothing else.

Charlotte wrote thus to Ellen Nussey a fortnight after Branwell's death:

The past three weeks have been a dark interval in our humble home. Branwell's constitution had been failing fast all the summer, but still neither the doctor nor himself thought him so near his end as he was. He was entirely confined to his bed but for one single day, and was in the village two days before his death.

The end came after twenty minutes' struggle on Sunday morning,

24th September. He was perfectly conscious till the last agony came on. His mind had undergone the peculiar change which frequently precedes death. Two days previously the calm of better feelings filled it. A return of natural affection marked his last moments. He is in God's hands now, and the All-Powerful is likewise the All-Merciful. A deep conviction that he rests at last – rests well after his brief, erring, suffering, feverish life – fills and quiets my mind now.

The final separation – the spectacle of his pale corpse – gave more acute, bitter pain than I could have imagined. Till the last hour comes, we never know how much we can forgive, pity, regret a near relation. All his vices were and are nothing now – we remember only his woes.

Papa was acutely distressed at first, but on the whole has borne the event well. Emily and Anne are pretty well, though Anne is always delicate, and Emily has a cold and cough at present.

Charlotte also wrote to her publisher, W. S. Williams, about her brother's death.

When I looked on the noble face and forehead of my dead brother (Nature had favoured him with a fairer outside, as well as a finer constitution than his sisters) and asked myself what had made him go ever wrong, tend ever downwards, when he had so many gifts to induce to, and aid in an upward course – I seemed to receive an oppressive revelation of the feebleness of humanity; of the inadequacy of even genius to lead to true greatness if unaided by religion and principle. In the value, or even the reality of these two things he would never believe till within a few days of his end, and then all at once he seemed to open his heart to a conviction of their existence and worth. The remembrance of this strange change now comforts my poor Father greatly. I myself, with painful, mournful joy, heard him praying softly in his dying moments, and to the last prayer which my father offered up at his bedside, he added 'amen'. How unusual that word appeared from his lips – of course you who did not know him, cannot conceive. Akin to this alteration was that in his feelings towards his relatives – all bitterness seemed gone.

When the struggle was over – and a marble calm began to succeed the last dread agony – I felt as I had never felt before that there was peace and forgiveness for him in Heaven. All his errors – to speak plainly – all his vices seemed nothing to me in that moment; every wrong he had done, every pain he had caused, vanished; his sufferings only were remembered; the wrench to the natural affections only was felt. If Man can thus experience total oblivion of his fellow's imperfections – how much more can the Eternal Being who made man, forgive his creature! Had his sins been scarlet in their dye – I believe now they are white as wool – He is at rest – and that comforts us all – long before he quitted this world Life had no happiness for him.

Emily's poem *The Wanderer from the Fold* is perhaps a more tender and forgiving response to Branwell's death.

The Wanderer from the Fold

How few, of all the hearts that loved,
    Are grieving for thee now;
And why should mine to-night be moved
    With such a sense of woe?

Too often thus, when left alone,
    Where none my thoughts can see,
Comes back a word, a passing tone
    From thy strange history.

Sometimes I seem to see thee rise,
    A glorious child again;
All virtues beaming from thine eyes
    That ever honoured men:

Courage and truth, a generous breast,
    Where sinless sunshine lay:
A being whose very presence blest
    Like gladsome summer-day.

Oh, fairly spread thy early sail,
    And fresh, and pure, and free
Was the first impulse of the gale
    Which urged life's wave for thee!

Why did the pilot, too confiding,
    Dream o'er that ocean's foam,
And trust in Pleasure's careless guiding
    To bring his vessel home?

For well he knew what dangers frowned,
    What mists would gather, dim;
What rocks, and shelves, and sand lay round
    Between his port and him.

The very brightness of the sun,
　　The splendour of the main,
The wind which bore him wildly on
　　Should not have warned in vain.

An anxious gazer from the shore –
　　I marked the whitening wave,
And wept above thy fate the more
　　Because – I could not save.

It recks not now, when all is over:
　　But yet my heart will be
A mourner still, though friend and lover
　　Have both forgotten thee!

The trees at Top Withens

5 Authorship and publication 1846-1848

Three years before Branwell died, the Brontë sisters had fortunately discovered a new interest and hope which undoubtedly sustained them through the terrible years of his decline. In her *Biographical Notice* prefixed to the edition of *Wuthering Heights* and *Agnes Grey* published in 1850 (and, therefore, after the deaths of both Emily and Anne) Charlotte gave a moving account of their publishing ventures.

BIOGRAPHICAL NOTICE

OF

ELLIS AND ACTON BELL

It has been thought that all the works published under the names of Currer, Ellis, and Acton Bell were, in reality, the production of one person. This mistake I endeavoured to rectify by a few words of disclaimer prefixed to the third edition of *Jane Eyre*. These, too, it appears, failed to gain general credence, and now, on the occasion of a reprint of *Wuthering Heights* and *Agnes Grey*, I am advised distinctly to state how the case really stands.

Indeed, I feel myself that it is time the obscurity attending those two names – Ellis and Acton – was done away. The little mystery, which formerly yielded some harmless pleasure, has lost its interest; circumstances are changed. It becomes, then, my duty to explain briefly the origin and authorship of the books written by Currer, Ellis, and Acton Bell.

About five years ago, my two sisters and myself, after a somewhat prolonged period of separation, found ourselves reunited, and at home. Resident in a remote district, where education had made little progress, and where, consequently, there was no inducement to seek social intercourse beyond our own domestic circle, we were wholly dependent on ourselves and each other, on books and study, for the enjoyments and occupations of life. The highest stimulus, as well as the liveliest pleasure we had known from childhood upwards, lay in attempts at literary composition; formerly we used to show each other what we wrote, but of late years this habit of communication and consultation had been discontinued; hence it ensued, that we were mutually ignorant of the progress we might respectively have made.

One day, in the autumn of 1845, I accidentally lighted on a MS. volume of verse in my sister Emily's handwriting. Of course, I was not surprised, knowing that she could and did write verse: I looked it over, and something more than surprise seized me – a deep conviction that these were not common effusions, nor at all like the poetry women generally write. I thought them condensed and terse, vigorous and genuine. To my ear they had also a peculiar music – wild, melancholy, and elevating.

My sister Emily was not a person of demonstrative character, nor one on the recesses of whose mind and feelings even those nearest and dearest to her could, with impunity, intrude unlicensed; it took hours to reconcile her to the discovery I had made, and days to persuade her that such poems merited publication. I knew, however, that a mind like hers could not be without some latent spark of honourable ambition, and refused to be discouraged in my attempts to fan that spark to flame.

Meantime, my younger sister quietly produced some of her own compositions, intimating that, since Emily's had given me pleasure, I might like to look at hers. I could not but be a partial judge, yet I thought that these verses, too, had a sweet, sincere pathos of their own.

We had very early cherished the dream of one day becoming authors. This dream, never relinquished even when distance divided and absorbing tasks occupied us, now suddenly acquired strength and consistency: it took the character of a resolve. We agreed to arrange a small selection of our poems, and, if possible, to get them printed. Averse to personal publicity, we veiled our own names under those of Currer, Ellis, and Acton Bell; the ambiguous choice being dictated by a sort of conscientious scruple at assuming Christian names positively masculine, while we did not like to declare ourselves women, because – without at that time suspecting that our mode of writing and thinking was not what is called 'feminine' – we had a vague impression that authoresses are liable to be looked on with prejudice; we had noticed how critics sometimes use for their chastisement the weapon of personality, and for their reward, a flattery, which is not true praise.

The bringing out of our little book was hard work. As was to be expected, neither we nor our poems were at all wanted; but for this we had been prepared at the outset; though inexperienced ourselves, we had read the experience of others. The great puzzle lay in the difficulty of getting answers of any kind from the publishers to whom we applied. Being greatly harassed by this obstacle, I ventured to apply to the Messrs Chambers, of Edinburgh, for a word of advice; *they* may have forgotten the circumstance, but *I* have not, for from them I received a brief and business-like, but civil and sensible reply, on which we acted, and at last made a way.

The book was printed: it is scarcely known, and all of it that merits to be known are the poems of Ellis Bell. The fixed conviction I held, and hold, of the worth of these poems has not indeed received the confirmation of much favourable criticism; but I must retain it notwithstanding.

Ill-success failed to crush us: the mere effort to succeed had given a wonderful zest to existence; it must be pursued. We each set to work on a prose tale: Ellis Bell produced 'Wuthering Heights', Acton Bell 'Agnes Grey', and Currer Bell also wrote a narrative in one volume. These MSS. were perseveringly obtruded upon various publishers for the space of a year and a half; usually their fate was an ignominious and abrupt dismissal.

At last 'Wuthering Heights' and 'Agnes Grey' were accepted on terms somewhat impoverishing to the two authors; Currer Bell's book found acceptance nowhere, nor any acknowledgment of merit, so that something like the chill of despair began to invade her heart. As a forlorn hope, she tried one publishing house more – Messrs Smith, Elder and Co. Ere long, in a much shorter space than that on which experience had taught her to calculate – there came a letter, which she opened in the dreary expectation of finding two hard, hopeless lines, intimating that Messrs Smith, Elder and Co. 'were not disposed to publish the MS.', and, instead, she took out of the envelope a letter of two pages. She read it trembling. It declined, indeed, to publish that tale, for business reasons, but it discussed its merits and demerits so courteously, so considerately, in a spirit so rational, with a discrimination so enlightened, that this very refusal cheered the author better than a vulgarly expressed acceptance would have done. It was added, that a work in three volumes would meet with careful attention.

I was then just completing 'Jane Eyre', at which I had been working while the one-volume tale was plodding its weary round in London: in three weeks I sent it off; friendly and skilful hands took it in. This was in the commencement of September, 1847; it came out before the close of October following, while 'Wuthering Heights' and 'Agnes Grey', my sisters' works, which had already been in the press for months, still lingered under a different management.

They appeared at last. Critics failed to do them justice. The immature but very real powers revealed in 'Wuthering Heights' were scarcely recognized; its import and nature were misunderstood; the identity of its author was misrepresented; it was said that this was an earlier and ruder attempt of the same pen which had produced 'Jane Eyre'. Unjust and grievous error! We laughed at it at first, but I deeply lament it now. Hence, I fear, arose a prejudice against the book.

Within a year of publication confusion over the identities of the authors of these three first novels had become so embarrassing that Charlotte and Anne felt that it was necessary for them to reveal their true identities to Charlotte's publishers. She writes to her friend, Mary Taylor, to tell her of their visit to London for this purpose. . . .

About two months since I had a letter from my publishers – Smith and Elder – saying that *Jane Eyre* had had a great run in America, and that a publisher there had consequently bid high for the first sheets of a new work by Currer Bell, which they had promised to let him have.

Presently after came another missive from Smith and Elder; their American correspondent had written to them complaining that the first sheets of a new work by Currer Bell had been already received, and not by their house, but by a rival publisher, and asking the meaning of such false play; it enclosed an extract from a letter from Mr Newby (A. and E. Bell's publisher) affirming that to the best of his belief *Jane Eyre*, *Wuthering Heights*, and *Agnes Grey*, and *The Tenant of Wildfell Hall* (the new work) were all the production of one author.

This was a *lie*, as Newby had been told repeatedly that they were the production of three different authors, but the fact was he wanted to make a dishonest move in the game to make the public and the trade believe that he had got hold of Currer Bell, and thus cheat Smith and Elder by securing the American publisher's bid.

The upshot of it was that on the very day I received Smith and Elder's letter, Anne and I packed up a small box, sent it down to Keighley, set out ourselves after tea, walked through a snowstorm to the station, got to Leeds, and whirled up by the night train to London with the view of

George Smith, publisher
of all Charlotte's novels

proving our separate identity to Smith and Elder, and confronting
Newby with his *lie*.

We arrived at the Chapter Coffee-House (our old place, Polly, we did
not well know where else to go) about eight o'clock in the morning. We
washed ourselves, had some breakfast, sat a few minutes, and then set off
in queer inward excitement to 65 Cornhill. Neither Mr Smith nor Mr
Williams knew we were coming – they had never seen us – they did not
know whether we were men or women, but had always written to us as
men.

We found 65 to be a large bookseller's shop, in a street almost as
bustling as the Strand. We went in, walked up to the counter. There were
a great many young men and lads here and there; I said to the first I could
accost: 'May I see Mr Smith?' He hesitated, looked a little surprised. We
sat down and waited a while, looking at some books on the counter,
publications of theirs well known to us, of many of which they had sent us
copies as presents. At last we were shown up to Mr Smith. 'Is it Mr

Smith?' I said, looking up through my spectacles at a tall young man. 'It is.' I then put his own letter into his hand directed to Currer Bell. He looked at it and then at me again. 'Where did you get this?' he said. I laughed at his perplexity – a recognition took place. I gave my real name: Miss Brontë. We were in a small room – ceiled with a great skylight – and there explanations were rapidly gone into; Mr Newby being anathematized, I fear, with undue vehemence. Mr Smith hurried out and returned quickly with one whom he introduced as Mr Williams, a pale, mild, stooping man of fifty, very much like a faded Tom Dixon. Another recognition and a long, nervous shaking of hands. Then followed talk – talk – talk; Mr Williams being silent, Mr Smith loquacious.

Mr Smith said we must come and stay at his house, but we were not prepared for a long stay and declined this also; as we took our leave he told us he should bring his sisters to call on us that evening. We returned to our inn, and I paid for the excitement of the interview by a thundering headache and harassing sickness. Towards evening, as I got no better and expected the Smiths to call, I took a strong dose of sal-volatile. It roused me a little; still, I was in grievous bodily case when they were announced. They came in, two elegant young ladies, in full dress, prepared for the Opera – Mr Smith himself in evening costume, white gloves, etc. We had by no means understood that it was settled we were to go to the Opera, and were not ready. Moreover, we had no fine, elegant dresses with us, or in the world. However, on brief rumination I thought it would be wise to make no objections – I put my headache in my pocket, we attired ourselves in the plain, high-made country garments we possessed, and went with them to their carriage, where we found Mr Williams. They must have thought us queer, quizzical-looking beings, especially me with my spectacles. I smiled inwardly at the contrast, which must have been apparent, between me and Mr Smith as I walked with him up the crimson-carpeted staircase of the Opera House and stood amongst a brilliant throng at the box door, which was not yet open. Fine ladies and gentlemen glanced at us with a slight, graceful superciliousness quite warranted by the circumstances. Still, I felt pleasantly excited in spite of headache and sickness and conscious clownishness, and I saw Anne was calm and gentle, which she always is.

The performance was Rossini's opera of the 'Barber of Seville', very brilliant, though I fancy there are things I should like better. We got home after one o'clock; we had never been in bed the night before, and had been in constant excitement for twenty-four hours. You may imagine we were tired.

6 Death of Emily and Anne 1848–1849

Three months after Charlotte and Anne had visited London in 1848, Branwell's end came and, within three months of his death, Emily, the author of *Wuthering Heights*, died. Charlotte's friend, Ellen Nussey, wrote the following appreciation of Emily's character and way of life at Haworth.

So very little is known of Emily Brontë every little detail awakens an interest. Her extreme reserve seemed impenetrable, yet she was intensely lovable. She invited confidence in her moral power. Few people have the gift of looking and smiling, as she could look and smile – one of her rare expressive looks was something to remember through life, there was such a *depth* of soul and feeling, and yet shyness of revealing herself, a strength of self-containment seen in no other – She was in the strictest sense a law unto herself, and a heroine in keeping to her law – She, and gentle Anne, were often seen twined together as united statues, of power and humility – they were to be seen with their arms lacing each other in their younger days whenever their occupation permitted their union. On the top of a moor or in a deep glen. Emily was a child in spirit for glee and enjoyment, or when thrown entirely on her own resources to do a kindness. She could be vivacious in conversation and enjoy giving pleasure – A spell of mischief also lurked in her on occasions, when out on the moors – She enjoyed leading Charlotte where she would not dare to go of her own free will – C. had a mortal dread of unknown animals and it was Emily's pleasure to lead her into close vicinity and then to tell her of what she had done, laughing at her horror with great amusement.

Emily did not easily make friends and it used to be a matter of surprise to Charlotte that she made an exception in my favour – She used to wish for my visits and was always kind and polite in her behaviour which was not often the case to other guests. Charlotte said she liked me because I never *seemed* to mark her peculiarities and I never pained her by treating her as a peculiar person. I remember after her death Charlotte spoke of Emily having valued me next to her sisters. This was the nearest approach she ever made I believe to anything like friendship apart. Anne and Emily were however very close friends, always together and in unison like dearly attached twins.

Emily was at home a very busy and industrious housekeeper doing all the ironing for the house and making all the bread. I remember books were a very common sight in the kitchen as I passed the open door, but their use never spoilt the bread, for I do not recollect such a thing as bad bread ever coming to table in all the years I visited Haworth.

If Emily wanted a book she might have left in the sitting-room she would dart in without looking at anyone, especially if any guest were present. Among the curates Mr Weightman was her only exception for any conventional courtesy. The ability with which she took up music was amazing, the style, the touch and the expression was that of a Professor absorbed heart and soul in his theme. The two dogs Keeper and Flossy were always in quiet waiting by the side of Emily and Anne during their Scotch breakfast of oatmeal and milk and always had a share handed down to them at the close of the meal.

Poor old Keeper! Emily's faithful friend and worshipper – he seemed to understand her like a human being – One evening when the four friends were sitting closely round the fire in C.'s sitting room – Keeper forced himself in between Charlotte and Emily and mounted himself on Emily's lap. Finding the space too limited for his comfort he pressed himself forward on to the guest's knee making himself quite comfortable – Emily's heart was won by the unresisting endurance of the visitor – little guessing that she herself being in close contact was the inspiring cause of submission to Keeper's preference. Sometimes Emily would delight in shewing off Keeper, make him frantic in action and roaring with the voice of a lion – it was a terrifying exhibition within the walls of an ordinary sitting room. Keeper was a solemn mourner at Emily's funeral and never recovered his cheerfulness.

A sad picture of Emily's death is offered us by Mary F. Robinson. She wrote the first biography of Emily Brontë, published in 1883 and it is likely that she took down the following narrative from Ellen Nussey.

The days drew on towards Christmas; it was already the middle of December and still Emily was about the house, able to wait upon herself, to sew for the others, to take an active share in the duties of the day. She always fed the dogs herself. One Monday evening, it must have been about the 14th of December, she rose as usual to give the creatures their supper. She got up, walking slowly, holding out in her thin hands an apronful of broken meat and bread. But when she reached the flagged passage the cold took her; she staggered on the uneven pavement and fell against the wall. Her sisters, who had been sadly following her, unseen, came forward, much alarmed and begged her to desist; but, smiling wanly, she went on and gave Floss and Keeper their last supper from her hands.

The next morning she was worse. Before her waking, her watching sisters heard the low unconscious moaning that tells of suffering continued even in sleep; and they feared for what the coming year might hold in store. Of the nearness of the end they did not dream. Charlotte had been out over the moors, searching every glen and hollow for a sprig of heather, however pale and dry, to take to her moor-loving sister. But Emily looked on the flower laid on her pillow with indifferent eyes. She was already estranged and alienate from life.

Nevertheless she persisted in rising, dressing herself alone, and doing everything for herself. A fire had been lit in the room, and Emily sat on the hearth to comb her hair. She was thinner than ever now – the tall, loose-jointed, 'slinky' girl – her hair in its plenteous dark abundance was all of her that was not marked by the branding finger of death. She sat on the hearth combing her long brown hair. But soon the comb slipped from her feeble grasp into the cinders. She, the intrepid, active Emily, watched it burn and smoulder, too weak to lift it, while the nauseous, hateful odour of burnt bone rose into her face. At last the servant came in: 'Martha,' she said, 'my comb's down there; I was too weak to stoop and pick it up.'

I have seen the old, broken comb with a large piece burned out of it, and have thought it, I own, more pathetic than the bones of the eleven thousand virgins at Cologne, or the time-blackened Holy Face of Lucca. Sad, chance confession of human weakness; mournful counterpart of that chainless soul which to the end maintained its fortitude and rebellion. The flesh is weak. Since I saw that relic, the strenuous verse of Emily Brontë's last poem has seemed to me far more heroic, far more moving; remembering in what clinging and prisoning garments that free spirit was confined.

The flesh was weak, but Emily would grant it no indulgence. She finished her dressing, and came very slowly, with dizzy head and tottering steps, downstairs into the little bare parlour where Anne was

Branwell's painting
of Emily

working and Charlotte writing a letter. Emily took up some work and tried to sew. Her catching breath, her drawn and altered face were ominous of the end. But still a little hope flickered in those sisterly hearts. 'She grows daily weaker,' wrote Charlotte on that memorable Tuesday morning; seeing surely no portent that this – this! was to be the last of the days and the hours of her weakness.

The morning drew on to noon and Emily grew worse. She could no longer speak, but – gasping in a husky whisper – she said: 'If you will send for a doctor, I will see him now!' Alas, it was too late. The shortness of breath and rending pain increased; even Emily could no longer conceal them. Towards two o'clock her sisters begged her, in an agony, to let them put her to bed. 'No, no,' she cried; tormented with feverish restlessness that comes before the last, most quiet peace. She tried to rise, leaning with one hand upon the sofa. And thus the cord of life snapped. She was dead. She was thirty years old.

Here are the last lines that Emily ever wrote:

> No coward soul is mine,
> No trembler in the world's storm-troubled sphere:
> I see Heaven's glories shine,
> And faith shines equal, arming me from fear.
>
> O God within my breast,
> Almighty, ever-present Deity!
> Life – that in me has rest,
> As I – undying Life – have power in thee!
>
> Vain are the thousand creeds
> That move men's hearts: unutterably vain;
> Worthless as withered weeds,
> Or idlest froth amid the boundless main,
>
> To waken doubt in one
> Holding so fast by thine infinity;
> So surely anchored on
> The steadfast rock of immortality.
>
> With wide-embracing love
> Thy spirit animates eternal years,
> Pervades and broods above,
> Changes, sustains, dissolves, creates, and rears.
>
> Though earth and man were gone,
> And suns and universes ceased to be,
> And Thou were left alone,
> Every existence would exist in Thee.
>
> There is not room for Death,
> Nor atom that his might could render void:
> Thou—THOU art Being and Breath,
> And what THOU art may never be destroyed.

On January 18th 1849, just one month after the death of Emily, Charlotte wrote to her publisher, W. S. Williams . . . .

MY DEAR SIR, – In sitting down to write to you I feel as if I were doing a wrong and selfish thing; I believe I ought to discontinue my correspondence with you till times change and the tide of calamity which of late days has set so strongly in against us, takes a turn. But the fact is, sometimes I feel it absolutely necessary to unburden my mind. To papa I must only speak cheeringly, to Anne only encouragingly, to you I may give some hint of the dreary truth.

Anne and I sit alone and in seclusion as you fancy us, but we do not study; Anne cannot study now, she can scarcely read; she occupies Emily's chair – she does not get well. A week ago we sent for a Medical Man of skill and experience from Leeds to see her; he examined her with the stethoscope; his report I forbear to dwell on for the present; even skilful physicians have often been mistaken in their conjectures.

My first impulse was to hasten her away to a warmer climate, but this was forbidden – she must not travel – she is not to stir from the house this winter – the temperature of her room is to be kept constantly equal.

Had leave been given to try change of air and scene, I should hardly have known how to act – I could not possibly leave papa – and when I mentioned his accompanying us the bare thought distressed him too much to be dwelt upon. Papa is now upwards of seventy years of age, his habits for nearly thirty years have been those of absolute retirement – any change in them is most repugnant to him and probably could not at this time especially – when the hand of God is so heavy upon his old age, be ventured upon without danger.

When we lost Emily I thought we had drained the very dregs of our cup of trial, but now when I hear Anne cough as Emily coughed, I tremble lest there should be exquisite bitterness yet to taste. However I must not look forwards, nor must I look backwards. Too often I feel like one crossing an abyss on a narrow plank – a glance round might quite unnerve.

So circumstanced, my dear Sir, what claim have I on your friendship – what right to the comfort of your letters? My literary character is effaced for the time – and it is by that only you know me – care of Papa and Anne is necessarily my chief present object in life to the exclusion of all that could give me interest with my Publishers or their connexions – Should Anne get better, I think I could rally and become Currer Bell once more – but if otherwise – I look no farther – sufficient for the day is the evil thereof.

Anne is very patient in her illness – as patient as Emily was unflinching. I recall one sister and look at the other with a sort of reverence as well as affection – under the test of suffering neither have faltered.

All the days of this winter have gone by darkly and heavily like a funeral train; since September sickness has not quitted the house – it is strange – it did not use to be so – but I suspect now all this had been coming on for years: unused any of us to the possession of robust health, we have not noticed the gradual approaches of decay; we did not know its symptoms; the little cough, the small appetite, the tendency to take cold at every variation of atmosphere have been regarded as things of course – I see them in another light now.

Anne's illness proved fatal, as Charlotte had realized. She survived the winter but by May of 1849 was very weak. It was decided that she should go to Scarborough to obtain such benefit from the sea-air as might alleviate her consumptive lungs. Charlotte and Ellen Nussey accompanied her and it is the latter who wrote this account of Anne's death.

On the 25th we arrived at Scarborough; our dear invalid having, during the journey, directed our attention to every prospect worthy of notice.

On the 26th she drove on the sands for an hour; and lest the poor donkey should be urged by its driver to a greater speed than her tender heart thought right, she took the reins and drove herself. When joined by her friend she was charging the boymaster of the donkey to treat the poor animal well. She was ever fond of dumb things, and would give up her own comfort for them.

On Sunday, the 27th, she wished to go to church, and her eye brightened with the thought of once more worshipping her God amongst her fellow creatures. We thought it prudent to dissuade her from the attempt, though it was evident her heart was longing to join in the public act of devotion and praise.

She walked a little in the afternoon, and meeting with a sheltered and comfortable seat near the beach, she begged we would leave her, and enjoy the various scenes near at hand, which were new to us but familiar to her. She loved the place, and wished us to share her preference.

The evening closed in with the most glorious sunset ever witnessed. The castle on the cliff stood in proud glory, gilded by the rays of the declining sun. The distant ships glittered like burnished gold; the little

Charlotte's
painting
of Anne

boats near the beach heaved on the ebbing tide, inviting occupants. The
view was grand beyond description. Anne was drawn in her easy chair to
the window, to enjoy the scene with us. Her face became illumined almost
as much as the glorious scene she gazed upon. Little was said, for it was
plain that her thoughts were driven by the imposing view before her to
penetrate forwards to the regions of unfading glory. She again thought of
public worship, and wished us to leave her, and join those who were
assembled at the house of God. We declined, gently urging the duty and
pleasure of staying with her, who was now so dear and so feeble. On

returning to her place near the fire she conversed with her sister upon the propriety of returning to their home. She did not wish it for her own sake, she said; she was fearing others might suffer more if her decease occurred where she was. She probably thought the task of accompanying her lifeless remains on a long journey was more than her sister could bear – more than the bereaved father could bear, were she borne home another and a third tenant of the family vault in the short space of nine months.

The night was passed without any apparent accession of illness. She rose at seven o'clock, and performed most of her toilet herself, by her expressed wish. Her sister always yielded such points, believing it was the truest kindness not to press inability when it was not acknowledged. Nothing occurred to excite alarm till about 11 a.m. She then spoke of feeling a change. 'She believed she had not long to live. Could she reach home alive, if we prepared immediately for departure?' A physician was sent for. Her address to him was made with perfect composure. She begged him to say 'how long he thought she might live – not to fear speaking the truth, for she was not afraid to die.' The doctor reluctantly admitted that the angel of death was already arrived and that life was ebbing fast. She thanked him for this truthfulness, and he departed to come again very soon. She still occupied her easy chair, looking so serene, so reliant: there was no opening for grief as yet, though all knew the separation was at hand. She clasped her hands, and reverently invoked a blessing from on high; first upon her sister, then upon her friend, to whom she said, 'Be a sister in my stead. Give Charlotte as much of your company as you can.' She then thanked each for her kindness and attention.

Ere long the restlessness of approaching death appeared, and she was borne to the sofa. On being asked if she were easier she looked gratefully at her questioner, and said, 'It is not *you* who can give me ease, but soon all will be well through the merits of our Redeemer.' Shortly after this, seeing that her sister could hardly restrain her grief, she said, 'Take courage, Charlotte; take courage.' Her faith never failed, and her eye never dimmed till about two o'clock, when she calmly, and without a sigh, passed from the temporal to the eternal. So still and so hallowed were her last hours and moments. There was no thought of assistance or of dread. The doctor came and went two or three times. The hostess knew that death was near, yet so little was the house disturbed by the presence of the dying, and the sorrow of those so nearly bereaved, that dinner was announced as ready, through the half-opened door, as the living sister was closing the eyes of the dead one. She could now no more stay the welled-up grief of her sister with her emphatic and dying 'Take courage,' and it burst forth in brief but agonizing strength. Charlotte's affection, however, had another channel, and there it turned in thought, in care, and in tenderness. There was bereavement, but there was not solitude; sympathy was at hand, and it was accepted. With calmness came the consideration of the removal of the dear remains to their home resting-place. This melancholy task, however, was never performed; for the afflicted sister decided to lay the flower in the place where it had fallen. She believed that to do so would accord with the wishes of the departed. She had no preference for place. She thought not of the grave, for that is but the body's gaol, but of all that is beyond it.

7 Charlotte experiences fame 1849–1852

After Anne's death, Charlotte was in a state of deep depression. She wrote to Ellen . . .

HAWORTH, July 14th 1849

I do not much like giving you an account of myself. I like better to go out of myself, and talk of something more cheerful. My cold, wherever I got it, whether at Easton or elsewhere, is not vanished yet. It began in my head; then I had a sore throat, and then a sore chest, with a cough, but only a trifling cough, which I still have at times. The pains between my shoulders likewise annoyed me much. Say nothing about it, for I confess I am too much disposed to be nervous. This nervousness is a horrid phantom. I dare communicate no ailment to papa; his anxiety harasses me inexpressibly.

My life is what I expected it to be. Sometimes when I wake in the morning, and know that Solitude, Remembrance, and Longing, are to be almost my sole companions all day through, that at night I shall go to bed with them, that they will keep me sleepless, that next morning I shall wake to them again; sometimes, Ellen, I have a heavy heart of it. But crushed I am not yet; nor robbed of elasticity, nor of hope, nor quite of endeavour. Still I have some strength to fight the battle of life. I am aware, and can acknowledge, I have many comforts, many mercies. Still I can *get on*. But I do hope and pray, that never may you, or any one I love, be placed as I am. To sit in a lonely room, the clock ticking loud through a still house, and to have open before the mind's eye the record of the last year, with its shocks, sufferings, losses, is a trial.

I write to you freely, because I believe you will hear me with moderation, that you will not take alarm or think me in any way worse off than I am. My love to your mother and sisters, and believe me yours sincerely,

C. B.

The endeavour to which Charlotte refers in that letter is
the completion of *Shirley*, her second major novel. With its
publication, later in 1849, and the gradual abandonment of the
carefully guarded secrecy surrounding the authorship of novels
by the Brontë sisters, Charlotte found herself moving far more
freely in society and meeting many leading literary figures. She
met the novelist Thackeray, whose daughter recollected an
evening when she came to dinner.

One of the most notable persons who ever came into our bow-
windowed drawing-room in Young Street is a guest never to be forgotten
by me – a tiny, delicate, little person, whose small hand nevertheless
grasped a mighty lever which set all the literary world of that day
vibrating. I can still see the scene quite plainly – the hot summer evening,
the open windows, the carriage driving to the door as we all sat silent and
expectant; my father, who rarely waited, waiting with us; our governess
and my sister and I all in a row, and prepared for the great event. We saw
the carriage stop, and out of it sprang the active, well-knit figure of Mr
George Smith, who was bringing Miss Brontë to see our father. My
father, who had been walking up and down the room, goes out into the
hall to meet his guests, and then, after a moment's delay, the door opens
wide, and the two gentlemen come in, leading a tiny, delicate, serious,
little lady, pale, with fair straight hair, and steady eyes. She may be a little
over thirty; she is dressed in a little *barège* dress, with a pattern of faint
green moss. She enters in mittens, in silence, in seriousness; our hearts
are beating with wild excitement. This, then, is the authoress, the
unknown power whose books have set all London talking, reading,
speculating; some people even say our father wrote the books – the
wonderful books. To say that we little girls had been given *Jane Eyre* to
read scarcely represents the facts of the case; to say that we had taken it
without leave, read bits here and read bits there, been carried away by an
undreamed-of and hitherto unimagined whirlwind into things, times,
places, all utterly absorbing, and at the same time absolutely
unintelligible to us, would more accurately describe our state of mind on
that summer's evening as we look at Jane Eyre – the great Jane Eyre – the
tiny little lady. The moment is so breathless that dinner comes as a relief
to the solemnity of the occasion, and we all smile as my father stoops to
offer his arm; for, though genius she may be, Miss Brontë can barely
reach his elbow. My own personal impressions are that she is somewhat
grave and stern, especially to forward little girls who wish to chatter. Mr

George Smith has since told me how she afterwards remarked upon my father's wonderful forbearance and gentleness with our uncalled-for incursions into the conversation. She sat gazing at him with kindling eyes of interest, lighting up with a sort of illumination every now and then as she answered him. I can see her bending forward over the table, not eating, but listening to what he said as he carved the dish before him.

I think it must have been on this very occasion that my father invited some of his friends in the evening to meet Miss Brontë – for everybody was interested and anxious to see her. Mrs Crowe, the reciter of ghost-stories, was there. Mrs Brookfield, Mrs Carlyle, Mr Carlyle himself was present, so I am told, railing at the appearance of cockneys upon Scotch mountain sides; there were also too many Americans for his taste, 'but the Americans were as gods compared to the cockneys,' says the philosopher. Besides the Carlyles, there were Mrs Elliott and Miss Perry, Mrs Procter and her daughter, most of my father's habitual friends and companions. In the recent life of Lord Houghton I was amused to see a note quoted in which Lord Houghton also was convened. Would that he had been present – perhaps the party would have gone off better. It was a gloomy and a silent evening. Every one waited for the brilliant conversation which never began at all. Miss Brontë retired to the sofa in the study, and murmured a low word now and then to our kind governess, Miss Truelock. The room looked very dark, the lamp began to smoke a little, the conversation grew dimmer and more dim, the ladies sat round still expectant, my father was too much perturbed by the gloom and the silence to be able to cope with it at all. Mrs Brookfield, who was in the doorway by the study, near the corner in which Miss Brontë was sitting, leant forward with a little commonplace, since brilliance was not to be the order of the evening. 'Do you like London, Miss Brontë?' she said; another silence, a pause, then Miss Brontë answers, 'Yes and No,' very gravely.

From *Chapters from Some Memories*, by Annie Thackeray Ritchie

In the next few years, visits to London and to stay with friends, such as Mrs Gaskell, became more frequent for Charlotte although, as this letter to Laetitia Wheelwright shows, they were always stressful, taking their toll of Charlotte's delicate constitution.

HAWORTH, KEIGHLEY, December 17th, 1849
MY DEAR LAETITIA, – I have just time to save the post by writing a brief

note. I reached home safely on Saturday afternoon, and, I am thankful to say, found papa quite well.

The evening after I left you passed better than I expected. Thanks to my substantial lunch and cheering cup of coffee, I was able to wait the eight o'clock dinner with complete resignation, and to endure its length quite courageously, nor was I too much exhausted to converse; and of this I was glad, for otherwise I know my kind host and hostess would have been much disappointed. There were only seven gentlemen at dinner besides Mr Smith, but of these, five were critics – a formidable band, including the literary Rhadamanthi of the *Times*, the *Athenaeum*, the *Examiner*, the *Spectator*, and the *Atlas*: men more dreaded in the world of letters than you can conceive. I did not know how much their presence and conversation had excited me till they were gone, and then reaction commenced. When I had retired for the night I wished to sleep; the effort to do so was vain – I could not close my eyes. Night passed, morning came, and I rose without having known a moment's slumber. So utterly worn out was I when I got to Derby, that I was obliged to stay there all night.

The post is going. Give my affectionate love to your mamma, Emily, Fanny, and Sarah Anne. Remember me respectfully to your papa, and – Believe me, dear Laetitia, yours faithfully,

C. Brontë

1851 saw Charlotte in London visiting the Great Exhibition and meeting Thackeray again. She wrote home to her father:

112 GLOUCESTER TERRACE,
HYDE PARK, June 7th 1851

DEAR PAPA, – I was very glad to hear that you continued in pretty good health, and that Mr Cartman came to help you on Sunday. I fear you will not have had a very comfortable week in the dining-room; but by this time I suppose the parlour reformation will be nearly completed, and you will soon be able to return to your old quarters. The letter you sent me this morning was from Mary Taylor. She continues well and happy in New Zealand, and her shop seems to answer well. The French newspaper duly arrived. Yesterday I went for the second time to the Crystal Palace. We remained in it about three hours, and I must say I was more struck with it on this occasion than at my first visit. It is a wonderful place – vast, strange, new, and impossible to describe. Its grandeur does not consist in *one* thing, but in the unique assemblage of *all* things. Whatever human industry has created, you find there, from the great compartments filled with railway engines and boilers, with mill-machinery in full work, with splendid carriages of all kinds, with harness of every description – to the glass-covered and velvet-spread stands loaded with the most gorgeous work of the goldsmith and silversmith, and the carefully guarded caskets full of real diamonds and pearls worth hundreds of thousands of pounds. It may be called a bazaar or a fair, but it is such a bazaar or fair as Eastern genii might have created. It seems as if magic only could have gathered this mass of wealth from all the ends of the earth – as if none but supernatural hands could have arranged it thus, with such a blaze and contrast of colours and marvellous power of effect. The multitude filling the great aisles seems ruled and subdued by some invisible influence. Amongst the thirty thousand souls that peopled it the day I was there, not one loud noise was to be heard, not one irregular movement seen – the living tide rolls on quietly, with a deep hum like the sea heard from the distance.

The Great Exhibition of 1851

Mr Thackeray is in high spirits about the success of his lectures. It is likely to add largely both to his fame and purse. He has, however, deferred this week's lecture till next Thursday, at the earnest petition of the duchesses and marchionesses, who, on the day it should have been delivered, were necessitated to go down with the Queen and Court to Ascot Races. I told him I thought he did wrong to put it off on their account – and I think so still. The amateur performance of Bulwer's play for the Guild of Literature has likewise been deferred on account of the races. I hope, dear papa, that you, Mr Nicholls, and all at home continue well. Tell Martha to take her scrubbing and cleaning in moderation and not overwork herself. With kind regards to her and Tabby, – I am, your affectionate daughter,

C. Brontë

Mrs Gaskell also describes this lecture by Thackeray:

The lady who accompanied Miss Brontë to the lecture of Thackeray's alluded to says that, soon after they had taken their places, she was aware that he was pointing out her companion to several of his friends, but she hoped that Miss Brontë herself would not perceive it. After some time, however, during which many heads had been turned round, and many glasses put up, in order to look at the author of *Jane Eyre*, Miss Brontë said, 'I am afraid Mr Thackeray has been playing me a trick'; but she soon became too much absorbed in the lecture to notice the attention which was being paid to her, except when it was directly offered, as in the case of Lord Carlisle and Mr Monckton Milnes. When the lecture was ended Mr Thackeray came down from the platform, and making his way towards her asked her for her opinion. This she mentioned to me not many days afterwards, adding remarks almost identical with whose which I subsequently read in *Villette*, where a similar action on the part of M. Paul Emanuel is related.

As they were preparing to leave the room her companion saw with dismay that many of the audience were forming themselves into two lines, on each side of the aisle down which they had to pass before reaching the door. Aware that any delay would only make the ordeal more trying, her friend took Miss Brontë's arm in hers, and they went along the avenue of eager and admiring faces. During this passage through the 'cream of society' Miss Brontë's hand trembled to such a degree that her companion feared lest she should turn faint and be unable to proceed; and she dared not express her sympathy or try to give her strength by any touch or word, lest it might bring on the crisis she dreaded.

More characteristic perhaps of her life in these four years following the death of Anne were times of intense application and loneliness at Haworth. A friend of Mrs Gaskell has left a valuable description of the impression that Haworth and the household there might make on a visitor.

The village street itself is one of the steepest hills I have ever seen, and the stones are so horribly jolting that I should have got out and walked with W——, if possible, but, having once begun the ascent, to stop was out of the question. At the top was the inn where we put up, close by the church; and the clergyman's house, we were told, was at the top of the churchyard. So through that we went – a dreary, dreary place, literally *paved* with rain-blackened tombstones, and all on the slope; for at Haworth there is on the highest height a higher still, and Mr Brontë's house stands considerably above the church. There was the house before us, a small oblong stone house, with not a tree to screen it from the cutting wind; but how we were to get at it from the churchyard we could not see! There was an old man in the churchyard, brooding like a ghoul over the graves, with a sort of grim hilarity on his face. I thought he looked hardly human; however, he was human enough to tell us the way, and presently we found ourselves in the little bare parlour. Presently the door opened, and in came a superannuated mastiff, followed by an old gentleman very like Miss Brontë, who shook hands with us, and then went to call his daughter. A long interval, during which we coaxed the old dog, and looked at a picture of Miss Brontë, by Richmond, the solitary ornament of the room, looking strangely out of place on the bare walls, and at the books on the little shelves, most of them evidently the gift of the authors since Miss Brontë's celebrity. Presently she came in, and welcomed us very kindly, and took me upstairs to take off my bonnet, and herself brought me water and towels. The uncarpeted stone stairs and floors, the old drawers propped on wood, were all scrupulously clean and neat. When we went into the parlour again we began talking very comfortably, when the door opened and Mr Brontë looked in; seeing his daughter there, I suppose he thought it was all right, and he retreated to his study on the opposite side of the passage, presently emerging again to bring W—— a country newspaper. This was his last appearance till we went. Miss Brontë spoke with the greatest warmth of Miss Martineau, and of the good she had gained from her. Well! we talked about various things – the character of the people, about her solitude, etc. – till she left the room to help about dinner, I suppose, for she did not return for an age. The old dog had vanished; a fat curly-haired dog honoured us with his company for some time, but finally manifested a wish to get out, so we were left alone. At last she returned, followed by the maid and dinner, which made us all more comfortable; and we had some very pleasant conversation, in the midst of which time passed quicker than we supposed, for at last W—— found that it was half-past three, and we had fourteen or fifteen miles before us. So we hurried off, having obtained from her a promise to pay us a visit in the spring; and the old gentleman having issued once more from his study to say good-bye, we returned to the inn, and made the best of our way homewards.

Miss Brontë put me so in mind of her own 'Jane Eyre'. She looked smaller than ever, and moved about so quietly, and noiselessly, just like a little bird, as Rochester called her, barring that all birds are joyous, and that joy can never have entered that house since it was first built; and yet, perhaps, when that old man married, and took home his bride, and children's voices and feet were heard about the house, even that desolate crowded graveyard and biting blast could not quench cheerfulness and hope. Now there is something touching in the sight of that little creature entombed in such a place, and moving about herself like a spirit, especially when you think that the slight still frame encloses a force of strong fiery life, which nothing has been able to freeze or extinguish.

8 Charlotte's marriage and death 1852–1855

Villette was completed, published and well-received in spite of Charlotte's excessive feelings of uncertainty and the morbid depression that had surrounded its writing. Much of this novel and of *Shirley* is concerned with the problems facing a single woman striving for independence in male-dominated Victorian society. Charlotte had no doubt that she would die an old maid but this was not to be. It is in December 1852 that the courtship of the Rev Arthur Bell Nicholls, the curate at Haworth, first becomes a major concern in Charlotte's letters:

. . . On Monday evening Mr Nicholls was here to tea. I vaguely felt without clearly seeing, as without seeing, I have felt for some time, the meaning of his constant looks, and strange, feverish restraint. After tea I withdrew to the dining-room as usual. As usual, Mr Nicholls sat with papa till between eight and nine o'clock, I then heard him open the parlour door as if going. I expected the clash of the front-door. He stopped in the passage: he tapped: like lightning it flashed on me what was coming. He entered, he stood before me. What his words were you can guess; his manner, you can hardly realise, nor can I forget it. Shaking from head to foot, looking deadly pale, speaking low, vehemently yet with difficulty, he made me for the first time feel what it costs a man to declare affection where he doubts response.

The spectacle of one ordinarily so statue-like, thus trembling, stirred, and overcome, gave me a kind of strange shock. He spoke of sufferings he had borne for months, of sufferings he could endure no longer, and craved leave for some hope. I could only entreat him to leave me then and promise a reply on the morrow. I asked him if he had spoken to papa. He said, he dared not. I think I half led, half put him out of the room. When he was gone I immediately went to papa, and told him what had taken place. Agitation and anger disproportionate to the occasion ensued; if I

Charlotte
Brontë, painting
by George
Richmond, 1850

had *loved* Mr Nicholls and had heard such epithets applied to him as were used, it would have transported me past my patience; as it was, my blood boiled with a sense of injustice, but papa worked himself into a state not to be trifled with, the veins on his temples started up like whipcord, and his eyes became suddenly bloodshot. I made haste to promise that Mr Nicholls should on the morrow have a distinct refusal.

I wrote yesterday and got this note. There is no need to add to this statement any comment. Papa's vehement antipathy to the bare thought of any one thinking of me as a wife, and Mr Nicholls's distress, both give me pain. Attachment to Mr Nicholls you are aware I never entertained, but the poignant pity inspired by his state on Monday evening, by the hurried revelation of his sufferings for many months, is something galling and irksome. That he cared something for me, and wanted me to care for him, I have long suspected, but I did not know the degree or strength of his feelings. Dear Nell, good-bye. – Yours faithfully,

C. Brontë

Charlotte's husband
Arthur Bell
Nicholls. After
Charlotte's death
he remained at
the Parsonage with
Patrick Brontë

Mr Brontë remained obstinately opposed to the marriage for many months but was eventually won round . . .

HAWORTH, April 11th, 1854

DEAR ELLEN, – Thank you for the collar; it is very pretty, and I will wear it for the sake of her who made and gave it.

Mr Nicholls came on Monday, and was here all last week. Matters have progressed thus since July. He renewed his visit in September, but then matters so fell out that I saw little of him. He continued to write. The correspondence pressed on my mind. I grew very miserable in keeping it from papa. At last sheer pain made me gather courage to break it. I told all. It was very hard and rough work at the time, but the issue after a few days was that I obtained leave to continue the communication. Mr Nicholls came in January; he was ten days in the neighbourhood. I saw much of him. I had stipulated with papa for opportunity to become better acquainted. I had it, and all I learnt inclined me to esteem and affection. Still papa was very, very hostile, bitterly unjust.

I told Mr Nicholls the great obstacle that lay in his way. He has persevered. The result of this, his last visit, is, that papa's consent is gained, that his respect, I believe, is won, for Mr Nicholls has in all things proved himself disinterested and forbearing. Certainly I must respect him, nor can I withhold from him more than mere cool respect. In fact, dear Ellen, I am engaged.

Mr Nicholls, in the course of a few months, will return to the curacy of Haworth. I stipulated that I would not leave papa, and to papa himself I proposed a plan of residence which should maintain his seclusion and convenience uninvaded and in a pecuniary sense bring him gain instead of loss. What seemed at one time impossible is now arranged, and papa begins really to take a pleasure in the prospect.

For myself, dear Ellen, while thankful to One who seems to have guided me through much difficulty, much and deep distress and perplexity of mind, I am still very calm, very inexpectant. What I taste of happiness is of the soberest order. I trust to love my husband. I am grateful for his tender love to me. I believe him to be an affectionate, a conscientious, a high-principled man; and if, with all this, I should yield to regrets, that fine talents, congenial tastes and thoughts are not added, it seems to me I should be most presumptuous and thankless.

Providence offers me this destiny. Doubtless then it is the best for me. Nor do I shrink from wishing those dear to me one not less happy.

It is possible that our marriage may take place in the course of the summer. Mr Nicholls wishes it to be in July. He spoke of you with great kindness, and said he hoped you would be at our wedding. I said I thought of having no other bridesmaid. Did I say rightly? I mean the marriage to be literally as quiet as possible.

Do not mention these things just yet. I mean to write to Miss Wooler shortly. Good-bye. There is a strange half-sad feeling in making these announcements. The whole thing is something other than imagination paints it beforehand; cares, fears, come mixed inextricably with hopes. I trust yet to talk the matter over with you. Often last week I wished for your presence, and said so to Mr Nicholls, Arthur as I now call him, but he said it was the only time and place when he could not have wished to see you. Good-bye. – Yours affectionately,

C. Brontë

It was fixed that the marriage was to take place on June 29. Her two friends arrived at Haworth Parsonage the day before; and the long summer afternoon and evening were spent by Charlotte in thoughtful arrangements for the morrow, and for her father's comfort during her absence from home. When all was finished – the trunk packed, the morning's breakfast arranged, the wedding dress laid out – just at bedtime, Mr Brontë announced his intention of stopping at home while the others went to church. What was to be done? Who was to give the bride away? There were only to be the officiating clergyman, the bride and bridegroom, the bridesmaid, and Miss Wooler present. The Prayer Book was referred to; and there it was seen that the rubric enjoins that the minister shall receive 'the woman from her father's or *friend's* hand', and that nothing is specified as to the sex of the 'friend'. So Miss Wooler, ever kind in emergency, volunteered to give her old pupil away.

The news of the wedding had slipt abroad before the little party came out of church, and many old and humble friends were there, seeing her look 'like a snowdrop', as they say. Her dress was white embroidered muslin, with a lace mantle, and white bonnet trimmed with green leaves, which perhaps might suggest the resemblance to the pale wintry flower.

Mrs Gaskell

Charlotte was married on June 29th, 1854. Her letters give every indication of her having thoroughly enjoyed her honeymoon in Ireland and of her being very happy in her marriage. However, early in 1855 she wrote to Ellen:

I very much wish to come to Brookroyd, and I hope to be able to write with certainty and fix Wednesday the 31st January as the day: but the fact is, I am not sure whether I shall be well enough to leave home. At present I should be a most tedious visitor. My health has been really very good ever since my return from Ireland till about ten days ago, when the stomach seemed quite suddenly to lose its tone, indigestion and continual faint sickness have been my portion ever since. Don't conjecture, dear Nell, for it is too soon yet, though I certainly never before felt as I have done lately. I am rather mortified to lose my good looks and grow thin as I am doing, just when I thought of going to Brookroyd. Poor Joe Taylor! I still hope he will get better, but Amelia writes grievous, though not always clear or consistent accounts. Dear Ellen, I want to see you, and I hope I shall see you well. My love to all. – Yours faithfully,

C. B. Nicholls

. . . she was attacked by new sensations of perpetual nausea and ever-recurring faintness. After this state of things had lasted for some time she yielded to Mr Nicholls's wish that a doctor should be sent for. He came, and assigned a natural cause for her miserable indisposition – a little patience and all would go right. She, who was ever patient in illness, tried hard to bear up and bear on. But the dreadful sickness increased and increased, till the very sight of food occasioned nausea. 'A wren would have starved on what she ate during those last six weeks,' says one. Tabby's health had suddenly and utterly given way, and she died in this time of distress and anxiety respecting the last daughter of the house she had served so long. Martha tenderly waited on her mistress, and from time to time tried to cheer her with the thought of the baby that was coming. 'I dare say I shall be glad some day,' she would say; 'but I am so ill – so weary—.' Then she took to her bed, too weak to sit up.

Mrs Gaskell

On February 15th, Charlotte wrote to Laetitia Wheelwright. Mrs Gaskell quotes the letter and then brings the story of the lives of the Brontë sisters to a close:

A few lines of acknowledgement your letter *shall* have whether well or ill. At present I am confined to my bed with illness, and have been so for three weeks. Up to this period, since my marriage, I have had excellent health. My husband and I live at home with my father; of course I could not leave *him*. He is pretty well, better than last summer. No kinder, better husband than mine, it seems to me, there can be in the world. I do not want now for kind companionship in health and the tenderest nursing in sickness. Deeply I sympathise in all you tell me about Dr W. and your excellent mother's anxiety. I trust he will not risk another operation. I cannot write more now; for I am much reduced and very weak. God bless you all! – Yours affectionately,

C. B. Nicholls

I do not think she ever wrote a line again. Long days and longer nights went by; still the same relentless nausea and faintness, and still borne on in patient trust. About the third week in March there was a change; a low, wandering delirium came on; and in it she begged constantly for food and even for stimulants. She swallowed eagerly now; but it was too late. Wakening for an instant from this stupor of intelligence, she saw her husband's woe-worn face, and caught the sound of some murmured words of prayer that God would spare her. 'Oh!' she whispered forth, 'I am not going to die, am I? He will not separate us, we have been so happy.'

Early on Saturday morning, March 31, the solemn tolling of Haworth church bell spoke forth the fact of her death to the villagers who had known her from a child. . . .

Further reading

Novels:

Charlotte Brontë
Jane Eyre
Shirley
The Professor
Villette

Emily Brontë
Wuthering Heights

Anne Brontë
Agnes Grey
The Tenant of Wildfell Hall

Biographies:

BENTLEY, P. (1969) *The Brontës and Their World* Viking Press
GASKELL, E. (1858) *The Life of Charlotte Brontë* Smith & Elder
LANE, M. (1953) *The Brontë Story* Heinemann
PETERS, M. (1975) *Unquiet Soul, The Biography of Charlotte Brontë* Hodder & Stoughton
PINION, F. B. (1975) *A Brontë Companion* Macmillan
SHORTER, C. K. (1908) *The Brontës: Life and Letters* 2 vols Hodder & Stoughton

Acknowledgments

Fay Godwin 2–3, 79
The Brontë Society, photography M. K. Howarth 9, 11, 14, 19, 21, 23, 24, 25, 27, 31, 38, 39, 51, 57, 69, 73, 75, 84, 93, 106
National Portrait Gallery, London 35, 89, 105
The Brotherton Library 70, 71